PracticeSpot Guide to

Promoting your
Teaching Studio

Philip Johnston

1

Published by
PracticeSpot Press
PracticeSpot Pty Ltd
52 Pethebridge Street
Pearce ACT 2607
AUSTRALIA

Cover design by Whizzbang Art, Canberra
Printed in the United States of America

ISBN 0958190518

Acknowledgements

To my daughters Kate and Laura—an apology for writing another book that is yet again entirely unsuitable as a bedtime story. This is something I will fix one day.

An ongoing thank you to Henry Weber—for his astonishing work ethic, friendship, vision and enthusiasm, and his faith in the grand adventure that is PracticeSpot. Henry, there's plenty already to be proud of, but the best is yet to come.

And a special thank you to my mother, Christine, who, if you'll forgive the alliteration, has become the official PracticeSpot Press Proofreader. 170,000 words and counting—and I'm not owning up to how many typos, misspellings and howlers she has unearthed so far...

Also by Philip Johnston

• **The Practice Revolution:** Getting great results from the six days *between* lessons. ISBN 095819050X

(PracticeSpot Press 2002, 324 pp)

• **Not Until You've Done Your Practice** ISBN 0646-0265X

(1990, 1998 and 2000, 118 pp Illustrations by David Sutton)

PracticeSpot Press official website

http://www.practicespot.com

Over 1000 pages of free resources and information for music teachers and students, together with excerpts and information about other PracticeSpot Press books.

Contents

Introduction

Why this book was needed

And the hidden benefits of a full studio

• Reinvesting more back into your studio • Choosing who you take • When students leave • The option for higher fees • The big income gains from small fee rises • The ability to take time out • Greater flexibility when timetabling • Full force of word of mouth promotion • The holiday bonus • Epic studio recitals • Additional income streams

Why this book was needed

In theory, this book shouldn't exist.

Music has become an industry with formidable self-promotion powers, our newspapers devoting column *yards* — not inches — to concert announcements and reviews. Our CD racks are piled high with the world's greatest works, ensuring that classic masterpieces are no longer a delight available only to bejewelled nobility at *soirees*, but can be yours too for less than the cost of a meal at McDonalds.

And with each sunset, our children are soothed to sleep not just by mother-sung lullabyes, but by their own personal symphony orchestra playing *Adagios for Babies, Volume 1,* while their parents look for the tell-tale signs of The Mozart Effect.

> ## Our greatest problem should not be "How can I fill my schedule?" but "Where on earth am I going to *put* all these people?"

It should surprise no-one that our cities then wake the following morning to the mesmerizing *tek-tuk-tuk-tuk* of metronomes, and the mantra of Major Scales. In every zip code, in every neighborhood, in every town, village and cul-de-sac, there are children who want to learn to play, and people who can show them how. Music has simultaneously become too exciting to resist, and too accessible to ignore.

In short, there has probably never been a better time to be a music teacher.

Given this, why on earth would a book on studio promotion be necessary? With 63 million amateur musicians in the US alone, surely the very foundations of our studios should already be *shaking* from eager parents pounding on our doors.

Our greatest problem should not be "How can I fill my schedule?" but "where on earth am I going to *put* all these people?", as we stare horrified at the oncoming mass of students, like Mickey

Mouse contemplating endless advancing broomsticks in *The Sorcerer's Apprentice.* We shouldn't be buying books on studio promotion—we should be pulling the phone out of its socket to stop the incessant ringing, and cowering behind our music stands as the final hinge on our front door gives way, allowing hordes of insatiable students to pour through...

At least that's what's *supposed* to happen. But despite the unprecedented demand, there are plenty of music teachers whose studios are nowhere near capacity, and who are confused about how to change it.

The problem is that while the demand may be exciting, there is also an abundance of *supply.* You have to remember that as far as parents are concerned, you're not the only music teacher in town. In fact,

> **When your phone doesn't ring, it's not always because parents considered your studio and rejected it.**
>
> **It's usually because they never noticed it in the first place.**

you're probably not the only music teacher in your *street.* As a result, parents seeking tuition for their children are often bewildered by options, and have enormous difficulty in distinguishing one studio from another. They're all just numbers and names in the yellow pages, and selecting a studio is really just a big game of Teacher Lotto.

You can't afford to be karmic like that about your studio's growth. Coca Cola doesn't just place their products meekly on supermarket shelves and *wait* for them to be noticed amongst all the other soft drinks. Mercedes-Benz doesn't just put out a new model and *hope* that the world thinks it's great. They promote the living daylights out of their products, and ensure that they don't only stand out from the crowd—they *lead* the crowd. And so when the time comes to name five quality car manufacturers, Mercedes is probably going to be on our list, which is a little odd given that most of us have never actually driven one. But we've all seen the commercials.

The idea is that when parents have to play the great Sign-Up-For-Music-Lessons Card Trick of "choose a teacher...any teacher" (and it can feel like that to them when they are staring at fifty-two different ads in the Yellow Pages), your playing card should be bigger than the others in the pack, better designed, more professional in tone, filled with the promise of good things for their child and positively leaping out at them. They should be reaching for it before they're even *seen* the other cards.

Not only that, there should be something about your card that is somehow...familiar. That they have heard of your studio before, even if they can't put a finger on how.

In short, your studio needs to be impossible to miss. In the past, when your phone has refused to ring, it's not always because parents have considered your studio and rejected it. *It's usually because they never noticed it in the first place.*

Remember, you don't need everyone in town to sign up for lessons with you to fill your studio—you just need the flow of incoming students to slightly exceed the flow of outgoing. The rest is just arithmetic.

So if your studio numbers are static at the moment, it doesn't necessarily say bad things about your teaching. It simply means there is a delicate *balance* between those incoming and outgoing students. In other words, you're only a knife edge away from tipping the balance so that your studio will start to fill up.

This book is about tipping that balance, and tipping it hard.

The hidden benefits of a full studio

This entire book is founded on the premise that having a full studio is somehow a desirable end. But apart from the warm inner glow of feeling that you're in demand, how can a full schedule and healthy waiting list really transform things for you?

Unless you're clear on the answer to that question—and the answer goes well beyond mere financial advantages—there's no point in fussing about studio promotion. It's a bit like thinking about gym programs without first being convinced of the benefits of getting fit.

The short answer is that teaching is a completely different job for those whose studios are full—it's less stressful, it's filled with more opportunities, and it's a lot more fun. The end result is that you can actually come out of a day of teaching fifteen students less tired and more enthusiastic than you did when you only used to teach five.

So what are these changes that await? And why is it that teachers with full schedules are in such a powerful position?

1. Teachers with full studios can afford to reinvest more back into the studio itself.

Once your schedule is full, your studio won't just be bigger—you'll be able to support a *better* studio. Want to create a comprehensively stocked CD lending library for your students? Or pay for an extension to your home for a bigger, dedicated studio instead of teaching in your living room? Or purchase recording facilities so that your students can make

> **Once your schedule is full, your studio won't just be bigger—you'll be able to support a *better* studio.**

their own CDs? All these things are possible with the additional income that a full studio brings. In turn, this then makes your studio a more attractive place for prospective students, creating a cycle that serves only to make your waiting list even longer.

But it's not just about using these new resources to attract new students. These resources will make your job easier with the students you already have, providing exciting new lesson options that will help your retention rates.

Take a moment and work out what your income would be if your studio were filled to the lid right now. What would you do with the extra money? Look around your studio, and you'll get some great ideas.

2. Teachers with full studios can be more selective about who they take.

Instead of having to accept anyone who comes along, you can afford to take only those students that you really want to work with.

The end result? Your job is easier, and a lot more fun. You can filter your studio so that your week is filled with exciting students who *want* to be where they are. It's a far cry from struggling with tone-deaf and unmotivated students who, but for the fact that you have rent to pay, would never have been allowed through your door in the first place.

> **You can look forward to your job, because it's a great group of hand-picked kids you're working with.**

This also increases the standard across the studio, ensuring that you are better represented at competitions and auditions.

But most of all, you can wake up each day with that most rare of gifts in any career — looking *forward* to your job. Because it's a great group of hand-picked kids you're working with.

3. Teachers with full studios don't need to worry when students leave.

If your schedule has gaps, a student leaving means an instant drop in income—and for teachers of small studios it can feel like a body blow every time someone moves on. If, however, your studio is full to the point where you already have a waiting list, then a student leaving simply means that you replace them straight away with someone else.

This also means that you can afford to gently nudge students who are either ready to move on, or for whom lessons are no longer working. Smaller studios don't have this luxury—they need to cling to every student for as long as possible, and often it's well past the use-by date.

> **Smaller studios don't have this luxury—they need to cling to every student for as long as possible...**
>
> **...and often it's well past the use-by-date.**

The end result is that your studio will stay fresh, ensuring that your schedule is filled with enthusiastic and hard working students. They'll also know that they need to take any warning to "shape up" very seriously, conscious of the fact that there are another dozen students who would love their lesson time.

4. Teachers with full studios can charge higher fees.

Given that you are no longer concerned if you lose a few students, you can afford to increase your fees. The laws of supply and demand apply to music teaching as much as to any other business—in fact if your teaching studio is obviously one of the most sought after in town, callers will be *expecting* the fees to be a little higher than normal.

You still might elect not to put up your fees—but the point is, the option is there if you wish.

5. Teachers with full studios enjoy big income increases from small fee rises.

It's simple arithmetic. If you have ten students, and you put your weekly lesson rate up by one dollar, that's like giving yourself a pay rise of $400 per year.

If instead you have *sixty* students, then that same small increase will be worth an extra $2,400 to you—and this is on top of the fact that your income was six times as big to start off with.

> **...if your teaching studio is obviously one of the biggest in town, callers will be *expecting* the fees to be a little higher than normal.**

Once your studio is full, a little increase can go a long way, and handled properly, can actually add to the perception of your studio being a place of excellence in teaching. (See the chapter on setting appropriate fees on p. 44)

6. Teachers with full studios are in a stronger position to take time out for professional development or family.

When student numbers are tight, you can't automatically disappear for two weeks for a pedagogy conference, lest some of your students disappear too. With a waiting list to protect you, and a general atmosphere of a thriving studio, students not only are more understanding when you need to attend such events—they will perceive your participation as a virtue.

7. Teachers with full studios can expect greater flexibility from students when timetabling

Once your studio is in demand, you can be tougher when negotiating with students over less-than-ideal lesson times. Because parents will be conscious of how hard it is to get into your studio in the first place, they're likely to be more accommodating when it comes to available times.

This also has an impact on students who are already part of your studio. Instead of expecting you to change times whenever things become inconvenient for them, parents will be more prepared to juggle their own commitments. The message is clear — don't mess with the lesson time, because in a studio of your size, it cannot simply be assumed that another time can be found.

8. Teachers with full studios enjoy the full force of word of mouth promotion

Again, it's simple arithmetic. If you have sixty students, you have three times the word of mouth promotion going on than if you have only twenty students.

Which means you're likely to get three times the number of enquiries generated by recommendations. Again, it's a variation on the "success breeds success" principle, and is part of the reason that big studios only seem to get bigger.

9. Teachers with full studios are able to take more generous holidays.

The number of weeks that your studio is open each year *is completely up to you.* One of the advantages of being one of the biggest and best known studios in town is that you can create longer holidays for yourself without raising an eyebrow. My own studio teaches 37 weeks in the year instead of the usual 40, but parents who come to me

> **One of the advantages of being one of the biggest and best known studios in town is that you can create longer holidays for yourself without raising an eyebrow.**

know that 37 weeks in my studio is going to help their child a lot more than 40 weeks with a less successful teacher. They're prepared to forgo the extra three lessons each year to be part of the studio.

I then come back from the extra break recharged, refreshed and filled with new ideas and enthusiasm — and so I do a better job in those 37 weeks than I would have with 40 in any case.

10. Teachers with full studios are able to put on studio recitals that knock people's socks off.

You'll be able to hire better venues. You'll be able to get programs professionally printed. You'll have a guaranteed larger audience, so that even polite clapping will sound to performers like a thunderous ovation. And you're more likely to have not just one, but several of those rare talented students who can astonish parents and inspire your other students with their own performances.

> ## Your studio of 60 students quickly turns into an audience of *three hundred* if each student brings family and a friend or two.

Your studio of 60 students quickly turns into an audience of *three hundred* if each student brings family and a friend or two. It turns a mere concert into a powerful celebration of the fact that your studio is doing a great job, and that your students are fortunate to be part of it all. Lay on some champagne for the interval, and let the parents enthuse to each other about how they wouldn't want their child to be anywhere else.

11. Teachers with full studios are able to benefit from additional income streams.

If your studio is bringing in a little extra by selling sheet music to students, that extra goes up threefold if your studio is three times the size. What was just a little extra pocketmoney is now paying for you to upgrade your recording equipment.

It's also providing enough volume of sales to put you in a good position to negotiate a special discount with your music store. Sixty students could well mean two hundred music books have to be supplied to you from *somewhere* this year — your local store will be keen to ensure that the "somewhere" is them, and not their competition.

Aside from the issue of sheet music sales, if your waiting list is honestly becoming too big to manage, you have the option of bringing aboard an associate teacher to help with the demand.

They benefit from having access to the demand that your studio generates, and instant growth in their own student base that might have taken a decade otherwise. You benefit because they pay you a percentage of their fees—almost like a franchise arrangement. The very fact that you have an associate lends yet more credibility to your studio, helping bring in yet more students, and in time, you may consider bringing aboard a second associate...and so on.

After all, once you're full, you're full. If you can help fill somebody else up too, and derive some financial benefit from doing so, then everybody wins.

So what's next?

You need to reread the previous few pages regularly, and hold the outlined benefits clearly in your mind. What you're pursuing is a worthwhile and exciting end, and this book will help you make it all a reality. But like all worthwhile pursuits, the task ahead is going to challenge you, and things are not always going to go according to plan. These pages exist to remind you of what's at stake, and to help you keep moving forwards when stopping feels easier.

So where do we start? It's time to look at the single most important concept behind studio promotion.

It's time to meet your Lobby.

The power of your Lobby

Because first impressions are everything

• The power of your Lobby • So what exactly is your Lobby? • A look at two Lobbies in action • The surprising truth behind the Lobbies • Getting your Lobby right

The power of your Lobby

So why is it that some teachers always seem to be getting new enquiries, while others languish with spaces in their schedule? The knee-jerk response it to simply assert that it's because some teachers are better than others. It's true—some teachers *are* better than others—but there's not always a correlation between teaching excellence and studio size. There are plenty of first rate music teachers whose studios are nowhere near as full as they deserve to be.

> **No matter how glittering your credentials, nor how exciting your lessons, unless your studio's Lobby is compelling, your phone is not going to ring.**

These teachers may have had years of tertiary training—on top of thousands of hours of practice and development of their own craft.

They may be excellent performers in their own right, capable of playing some of the most demanding works in the repertoire.

They may have exciting ideas about teaching, relate well to their students, and conduct themselves professionally at all times.

It's completely irrelevant.

You may well have a great musical CV, but when parents are browsing through the yellow pages, looking for someone to teach their child, it's a different ball game entirely. In the end, no matter how glittering your credentials, nor how exciting your lessons, unless your studio's *Lobby* is compelling, your phone is not going to ring. Which means you'll never get a chance to show your abilities in the first place.

It's a huge jolt for most music teachers, but it's so important, that I will say it again:

No matter how glittering your credentials, nor how exciting your lessons, unless your studio's Lobby is compelling, your phone is not going to ring.

It's that simple. If you get your Lobby wrong, your studio will never fill up. Get it right, and you'll end up with a waiting list you can't jump over.

So if your studio is less full that you would like, don't doubt your teaching ability. Take a long hard look at your studio's Lobby instead.

The good news is that your Lobby is very, very easy to change. The hardest part is realizing that you need to.

So what exactly is your "Lobby"?

A hotel lobby communicates plenty about the standard—and standards—of the hotel itself, without the would-be guest even needing to check out a room. The lighting, the decor, the way you are spoken to, the other clientele, the sounds, the smells, the neighborhood—all contributing to your impression of the entire establishment, and to your decision as to whether or not you stay.

But in reality, the hotel's lobby was in action long before you set foot in there. The ads you read, the phone calls you made, the reviews you looked up all contributed to your decision to visit, and formed a part of a wider lobby.

> **Your Lobby is everything your students can find out about your studio short of actually having lessons with you.**

In fact, it could be argued that *any representation made of, or by, the hotel in public is part of their lobby.* Their website. Their stationery. Their grounds. Their telephone manner. Their mission statement. Their newspaper advertisement. Their feature in "Great Weekend Getaways" magazine. Their other hotels.

The essence of the hotel's business may well be the room itself. That's where you'll be staying for the night. But your decision to stay or not is based on dozens of small impressions—none of which were based on having actually seen the room.

In other words, the Lobby wasn't merely your first impression. It was the critical element in your decision to call in the first place.

Your Lobby is everything students can find out about your studio short of actually having a lesson with you. Like the hotel's lobby, it's made up of your advertising, your telephone manner, your stated ideals...and the dozens of other elements that go toward making up the public face of your studio.

It's not enough to simply be aware of the importance of your Lobby though. You have to be smart about how you construct it, and keenly aware of how it will be perceived.

A look at two Lobbies in action

Let's imagine for a moment that the radiator on your car is leaking, and you are looking to have it either repaired or replaced. Like many musicians, your knowledge of cars might end shortly after the steering wheel begins, but you've come across two advertisements in the Yellow Pages that might help—one is for "Bill's Auto Repairs", graphically slick with a map showing the location of the shop, testimonials from happy customers, and a web address for more information.

> **Al might be the best mechanic in town. But it's not going to matter, because chances are that he's not going to get the job.**

By contrast, the other is simply a couple of lines talking about "Al's Garage", listing a phone number, and with a misspelled motto: "Customer satisfaction garanteed"

Now don't get me wrong. Al might actually be the best mechanic in town. But it's not going to matter, because chances are that he's not going to get the job. And as we'll see, the poor ad is just part of the reason.

Let's assume that you decide to call both businesses to set up comparative quotes. Bill's Auto-repairs is answered by a receptionist, who puts you through to the relevant cooling systems expert. He spends ten minutes with you answering your questions on the phone, and generally being friendly and helpful, leaving you knowing more about radiators than you ever thought possible.

By contrast, calling "Al's Garage" just produces a nervous sounding answering machine message saying that Al is unavailable, and that he'll get back to you if you leave your name and number. You do, but he doesn't.

If this particular two-horse-race was not over at the point of reading the ads, it is now, and I don't need to ask you where you would take your business. Of course, that's only one side of the story though. The truth is a little more surprising than the ads would have you believe.

...the surprising truth behind the Lobbies

What the first ad *didn't* mention is that Bill's Auto Repairs has actually only been operating for three months, while Bill himself only just completed his apprenticeship. In fact, in the short history of his business, your radiator will be the very *first* he has worked on. The "receptionist" was simply his fiancée, who answers the phone at their home, and patches all calls through to Bill—who just happens to be the

> **As an uninformed consumer, our choice was not based on the quality of their work, but on the appearance of their Lobby...**
>
> **...the entry point and first contact you had with their business.**

"relevant expert" for all problems, from windscreen wipers to bald tyres. Far from being a multi-mechanic large scale operation with staff who specialize on different problems, Bill actually works alone. But the impression the ad and phone call gives is of a busy, thriving shop, filled with expert help.

By contrast, Al has been in the business for twenty-three years already. He *is* an expert. He's been repairing cars since he was a small kid, helping his dad renovate classic sports cars in the family shed. He probably already knows more about radiators than Bill is likely to discover in the next decade—which makes perfect sense,

31

since he was actually the master mechanic who took Bill through his apprenticeship. Twice "Apprentice of the Year" himself in days gone by, Al is quietly one of the best around, but stands by his father's conviction that advertising is overpriced and a waste of money.

His one sadness in a job that he otherwise enjoys is that he has been unable to grow his business a little more, although he knows plenty of fellow mechanics whose workshops are similarly quiet. Just the nature of the game, he laments. You don't become a mechanic if you want to earn a comfortable living.

> # It goes beyond first impressions.
>
> # If your lobby is anything less than compelling, *you won't get an opportunity for a second impression.*

Well we haven't helped Al any, because we ended up taking the car to Bill instead. As an uninformed consumer, this initial choice was not based on the quality of their work, *but on the appearance of their Lobby* — the entry point and first contact you had with their business. In this case, it was a Yellow Pages ad, and a telephone call.

None of us need be surprised to find out that within a few years, Bill's business was a multi-mechanic success story.

When the rest of this book starts unleashing various promotion ideas for your studio, they're all aimed at one thing — making your Lobby compelling. Because like our scenario above, most potential students actually know very little about music lessons, and Lobbies are all they will have to assess different studios.

Which is why you need to make yours memorable.

Getting your Lobby right

The concept of a "Lobby" is not just important to understand, it's *central* to promoting any service based enterprise — in fact, as far as potential students go, your Lobby *is* your business. Assumptions about the quality of your studio have to be based around that entry point, because at that early stage, *prospective students have no other information to work with.*

I cannot overstate how important this idea is. It has to go beyond the familiar warning about "first impressions", because if your Lobby is anything less than compelling, *you won't get an opportunity for a second impression.* There will be no phone call, there will be no interview, and no matter how great a teacher you are, there will be no lessons.

That's where this book can help. It's packed with ideas to help you build a compelling lobby, and ensuring that your Lobby then *evolves* to keep your studio at the forefront of parents' considerations.

Getting Started

Taking your first steps towards a bigger studio

• Taking stock • Creating your Future Teaching Schedule • Setting the right fee • Improving your desktop publishing skills • Your voicemail message • The qualification edge

Taking stock

When teachers worry about their studios not being full, the first thing I tell them to do is to write down *everything* they have done in the last twelve months to promote their studio. No elaborations, just bullet points and an item by item summary — the idea being to ensure that you cannot delude yourself by padding. So instead of writing:

> • At the beginning of the year, I took out a Yellow Pages ad, in order to promote my studio effectively to those who use the Yellow Pages as a reference point, and to increase the chances of receiving enquiries from that source.

Most music teachers are so busy actually *teaching* that they don't allocate anywhere near enough time or resources to studio promotion.

Simply put:

• Yellow Pages ad

Right now, before you read any more of this book, get a sheet of paper and a pencil, and make your own list. Write down absolutely everything that you have done in the last year specifically to promote your studio. Take plenty of time to make sure you haven't left anything out, then come back.

§

§

No, I'm serious. Really go and do it. I'll be waiting here when you get back. I have a cup of coffee and a magazine to read, I'll be fine. We both need to take a look at that list before we go any further.

Don't turn this page until you're finished.

§

Your list

All done? Ok, let me take a look. Give me a second here...wow, your handwriting is as bad as mine...

... ok. I think I've found the problem.

Just *there* on your page. No, not up there, you're looking in the wrong place—you won't find the problem in any of the things you wrote.

It's the space underneath. The things you *didn't* write. The things you couldn't write because they never happened in the first place.

So why is there so much space?

It's nothing you should feel bad about. It's simply that most music teachers are so busy actually *teaching* that they don't allocate anywhere enough time or resources to studio promotion. They ignore it because it just doesn't feel like it's related to music—promotion is certainly not what our conservatorium past trained us to think about.

> **Put the list away in a safe place. It's now officially a relic from the way you used to do things.**

More than that, dedicating time to advertising your studio just doesn't seem like Art. It feels somehow...unseemly...more like something that a small business would have to do.

Well guess what. You *are* running a small business. And unless you actively promote it, your business will *stay* very small.

Now what?

If your list looks short, don't worry—almost everybody else's is too. We've all done Harmony and Counterpoint 101, but very few of us have done Marketing 101. As a result, that space at the bottom of the page is typical of most music studios, and is the reason that so many teachers struggle to build healthy waiting lists in the first place.

It has nothing to do with the quality of your teaching. There are brilliant teachers whose studios are smaller than they should be, simply because their promotion list ends almost as soon as it begins.

This book is going to help you fill that list, so that you can fill your studio. It will introduce you to studio promotion ideas that you have never considered before, and will help you fine tune the promotion techniques you already use.

In the meantime, put the list away in a safe place. It's now officially a relic from the way you used to do things — and a warning that if you keep doing what you've been doing, you'll keep getting what you've been getting. All of which leads neatly to your next task.

Create a copy of your Future Teaching Schedule

Having come to terms with your past, it's time to get excited about your future. To do this, we're going to need a copy of your teaching schedule, but I'm not talking about the teaching schedule you currently have. I'm talking about the one you *wish* you had.

Fill it with dummy names and times—don't worry too much about how such a schedule could become a reality. If you currently only have seven students, but wish you had seventy, then seventy it is. It *is* achievable, and writing it out like this is an important first step.

> **If you currently only have seven students, but wish you had *seventy*, then seventy it is.**

There's an example on the next page of a sixty student timetable—the names come from a random name generator that I found on the web. You'll notice that the schedule includes breaks, days off, and a reflection of the fact that most students are at school or work between 9 am and 3 pm. In other words, you want your Future Teaching Schedule to appear *as realistic as possible*, because for your studio promotion campaign to begin in earnest, you have to believe that the schedule is attainable. It's no good filling in a schedule with one hundred and thirty students that have you teaching from 7 am to 8 pm every day with no breaks—you'll never believe what you're looking at. (Quite apart from anything else, no teacher could sustain a workload like that!)

The next step is then to put that schedule where you're going to see it every day. Next to your bathroom mirror. On your fridge. Near your phone. Beside your alarm clock. In fact, you should make more than one copy—you want this schedule to be in your face regularly.

So how does it help? That schedule has become a tangible manifestation of your goal. It's one thing to simply say "I wish my studio were bigger". It's quite another to be able to *see* it for yourself. Now all you need to do is go make it happen — a task that will actually feel more real and achievable for having seen what you're aiming at.

Future Teaching Schedule
60 students

	MON	TUE	WED	THUR	FRI	SAT
8:00 am	Andrew **Gilliam**	Kurt **Giltner**	Max **Gabriele**	Fannie **Kramer**	Neil **Lichty**	
8:30 am	Karen **Hampton**	Donna **Yeager**	Shannon **Dixon**	Howard **Smith**	Dorthey **Pierce**	
9:00 am	Victor **Flynn**	Alice **Holiday**	Jennifer **Douglas**	Cody **Pletcher**	Lonnie **Rolen**	
2:30 pm	Darren **Segarra**	Emily **Ingram**	Althea **Delcid**	Ernie **Hampton**	Kelly **Paxson**	Diane **Edwards**
3:00 pm	Mary Jane **Adams**	Fernando **Slaugh**	Kelly **Patchett**	Guy **Hyche**	Lakisha **Albseron**	Annette **Cavene**
3:30 pm	Roslyn **Somma**	Gerald **Clark**	Annette **Smith**	Kurt **Silvero**	Clare **Forbush**	Bob **Adams**
4:00 pm	Sally **Lim**	Jami **Drewes**	Lawrence **Ward**	Ashlee **Tengan**	Neil **Bassin**	
4:30 pm	Coy **Ayars**	Erik **Kellems**	Nelson **Forshee**	Ted **Ruddy**	Ted **Prodaska**	
5:00 pm	*BREAK*	*BREAK*	*BREAK*	*BREAK*	*BREAK*	
5:30 pm	Jamal **Jenkins**	Diane **Schroder**	Lakisha **Klarkin**	Reginald **Nichols**	Hugh **Ryer**	
6:00 pm	Jessie **Matsuo**	Lenore **Beegle**	Victor **Jenkins**	Nita **Penning**		
6:30 pm	Hillary **Hollens**	Matthew **Hebb**	Saundra **Viruet**	Jamie **Patnode**		
7:00 pm	Matthew **Vena**	Clayton **Sheroan**	Jessie **Tester**	Kristi **Kinley**		

When I first wrote out my own future teaching schedule, I had eighteen students. The simple act of looking at the "full" timetable every day produced regular bursts of activity, and the feeling that the goal itself was real, and therefore achievable. Confronted with the carrot on the end of the stick, I was constantly prompted into action with thoughts of "what can I do to make this a reality?" — ideas that never would have occurred to me otherwise.

Within eighteen months, I had *seventy* students in the studio, and a waiting list to boot — which is exactly what my future schedule outlined. There's no magic involved. It's just the combination of a clear target, and taking small but regular steps towards it.

If I had simply let things run without this intervention, I doubt very much that I would have reached thirty students in the same time frame.

Adjusting for reality

Before you become too attached to your Future Teaching Schedule, you need to ensure that you would be able to cope with such a timetable were it to become a reality. Remember, once you allocate those times to teaching, you cannot use them for anything else. Viewed in this light, you'll probably want to make some adjustments to your projection.

> **If you use the ideas in this book well, you will end up with the studio you are wishing for, so wish carefully.**

For example, the fact that you've scheduled students for a Saturday may look fine on paper, but it's not so good if your family likes to go camping on the weekends. You either need to schedule fewer students, or reschedule your Saturday students to early weekday evenings. Similarly, a stroke of a pen would be all you need to schedule three students before 9 am each day for a whopping fifteen student bonus, but that's no good if you spend most of those early mornings gripping a cup of coffee as you stumble into furniture with your eyes half closed. If you're genuinely not a morning person, then it's no good having an early-bird timetable, no matter how many extra students it provides on paper.

The traditional warning has always been "Be careful what you wish for — you might get it". If you use the ideas in this book well, you will end up with the studio you are wishing for, so wish carefully. But that caution aside, put your Future Teaching Schedule somewhere safe — it's a major part of the campaign ahead.

What's next?

Armed now with a clear goal, and a tangible way of being regularly reminded of that goal, it's time to look at an issue that can have a greater impact on student numbers than all your qualifications combined.

Pricing.

We'll look at where to set your fees, and why most teachers get this badly wrong.

Setting the right fee

It's one of the toughest decisions you'll have to make, but is one that can have a tremendous bearing on your ability to attract students. How much should you charge for the lessons you provide?

The temptation is to keep the price low, particularly if your studio is establishing itself. To ensure that when people call you, they are pleasantly surprised by how modest your fees are compared with other teachers they may have spoken to.

> **The temptation is to keep your price low...don't fall for this.**
>
> **Setting your fees too low is one of the *worst* things you can do to promote your studio.**

Don't fall for this. Setting your price too low is one of the *worst* things you can do to promote your studio. You have to remember, you are a service provider, not a retailer, and when people hear your price, *they will make assumptions about the quality of your service.* So if your lessons are $8 for half an hour, when most other people seem to be charging $15, the caller will start to wonder why you're so cheap.

In fact, if most other people with similar qualifications to you are charging $15, you should be charging *$17.* Your price is part of your lobby, and the ticket will sometimes say more to prospective students about your studio than all your copy writing combined.

Think how you would react as a potential client. Let's assume that you were getting your house painted. Most quotes came in at around $1500. One comes in at $950. Another at $1700. Ask yourself right now — who do you think the best painter is likely to be? Knowing nothing about them except the price, it's hard to shake the feeling that if you wanted the best job possible, you should at least *talk* to the painter that charges the most.

Whether or not you actually go for the $1700 job is a separate question, and might be a function of your own financial limitations, but the fact will remain that *part of you will wish you could have afforded the premium service* — and if you go with a cheaper option, every tiny blemish will have you regretting that you didn't spend the extra.

Well guess what. Parents who are conscientious enough to be contemplating music lessons in the first place are usually conscientious enough to want a first rate job, and they'll be quite prepared to pay a couple of extra dollars per lesson to make it happen.

And those odd parents who are think they can save a couple of bucks by going somewhere else? You're better off without them. When the first question I hear from a parent is "how much are the lessons?", I have lost interest already, because I know their priorities are suspect.

Reinvesting your gains

Charging appropriate fees has a powerful benefit that goes well beyond first impressions of quality. The higher fees represents additional resources, which, if invested back into your business, will help your studio grow at a much faster rate than you ever would have thought possible.

Reinvesting your time

By extra resources, I don't just mean extra money. If your fees are 25% higher than you first intended, then you would only need four students to bring in income that you used to need *five* students to produce. Doesn't sound so exciting in a studio of four students, but if there are thirty two students in your studio, that suddenly means *additional income from eight students that you don't actually have to teach.* I'm sure you'll have no trouble thinking of how you could spend the four spare hours you would have each week.

Still not convinced? In the course of a forty week teaching year, those four hours add up to 160 hours of additional free time — only a few hours short of a whole *week*! It's enough time to pursue some extra qualifications, or write articles for newspapers, or any of the dozens of other more time intensive promotion activities outlined later in this book. So while you're welcome to use the extra time lying in a hammock, sipping drinks with umbrellas in them, you should think about reinvesting a substantial slice of that time into promoting your studio.

Reinvesting your additional income

The other way of looking at higher fees is not in terms of extra time, but in terms of the extra income it represents—*and to then look at investing that extra income straight back into your business.* So instead of looking at lifestyle improvements from your higher fees, use them to purchase exciting new facilities for the studio itself, or that high impact Yellow Pages ad you thought you couldn't afford.

In this way, your additional income translates directly into an improved capacity to attract new students—helping ensure that your studio continues to grow for years to come. In this game, like any other, success breeds success, and the pain of investing into your studio will be quickly forgotten when you see the impact it has on your future student numbers.

And remember, if your studio grows enough, you are in a strong position to put fees up again, and so the cycle continues.

A caution

While this principle of reinvesting a percentage of a healthy fee back into the studio is a sound recipe for growth, you can't stretch the logic and decide "Wow! If I put up my fees 100%, then I would only need to teach *half* as many students!".

There has to be a sensitivity to two things before you start charging $500 an hour:

Being aware of what your competitors charge

While your fees can certainly be higher, they do need to be in the same ball park as other equivalently qualified or resourced teachers. As long as you are within a few dollars per lesson, then you're in the hunt, and in conjunction with the fact that your Lobby will be more compelling than theirs (see the next section of this book), should see you leading the pack. But if you are suddenly *$10* a lesson more expensive than your competitors, then your promotion campaign is going to have to be very slick for the gap to be perceived as worthwhile.

So how do you find out what your competitors charge? That's easy enough—simply call up (or have a relative call up) and pretend to be a student. Not only can you learn about their fees, but you can learn a thing or two about their telephone manner in the process. If you hear a great way of handling one of your questions, write it down.

There's nothing wrong with a little industrial espionage.   (In fact, later in this book, there are some tactics that all but recommend it)

Being sensitive to the students you already have

Even if it's now clear to you that your fees are way too low, you can't suddenly hit your current students with a brand new bill. Otherwise you might find yourself with a lot more spare time than you intended.

You either have to view the increase as an incremental exercise over several years, or you'll have to establish that the new rate applies to new students only. In fact, an announcement to parents that fees have gone up, *but not for them*, can generate tremendous goodwill among your existing students—almost like a loyalty bonus. You normally have to be very careful about charging different students different rates, but a date-based cutoff like this is discriminatory in a way that nobody can take offence to.

What's next?

Whether it's a newspaper advertisement, Yellow Pages ad, or sponsorship notice for a local theatre company, almost all your promotion ideas will have some element of written communication involved. Unless you have a graphic design team on standby, you're going to need to brush up on your Desktop Publishing Skills—and it's much easier than you think.

Improve your desktop publishing skills

In years gone by, one of the biggest advertising costs was actually paying to have material designed and printed. Now you can easily and cheaply do it yourself with a PC and a printer—but you have to know what you're doing, otherwise your new ad can look like a title page for a fourth grader's science project.

> **No matter how impressive the content, if your material is laid out badly, the result is guaranteed...**
>
> **...people won't read it in the first place.**

If that doesn't worry you, it should. No matter how impressive the content, if your material is laid out badly, the result is guaranteed—people won't read it in the first place.

It's not just the high impact brochures and newspaper advertisements that will benefit from solid desktop publishing skills. Every piece of written correspondence you create leaves an impression about your studio—from invoices, to your business card, to newsletters, to thank-you notes to strategic business partners. You will make use of these skills dozens of times every year, for decades to come, making it one of the most effective upgrades you can give yourself. And given that the written word is the most likely way people will encounter your Lobby for the first time, it's something you have to get right.

The essential tools

You can do a lot just with Microsoft Word, but if you're serious about creating good looking Yellow Pages ads, fliers, brochures or newspaper ads, you need specialist layout software—at the very least Microsoft Publisher, but preferably Adobe Pagemaker or

Indesign. The latter two will not only allow you to easily rearrange all your material on the page, but will also allow you to export the ad in a format that other print professionals will be able to work with—meaning that you can have total control over the layout of your Yellow Pages or newspaper advertisement. You supply the file, they print it, no fiddling required, which means you won't suddenly be confronted with spelling mistakes, or fonts that you didn't want. For better or for worse, the ad will look *exactly* as you intended it to.

Layout software can be expensive, but again, it's an investment that represents exciting extra options for you, and you will save money by not having to outsource the creation of your brochures and other printed advertisements. But more importantly, the fact that your advertisements consistently *look* professional will help attract students. No matter how expensive the software, just one new student would very quickly cover the cost—something that a lot of teachers forget when ruling out such assets.

> **The simple fact that your advertisements consistently *look* professional will help attract students.**

Of course, simply *having* the software is only a start.

Becoming proficient

While it's not hard to use layout software, there is an art to using it well. Check to see if there are any short courses running in layout and desktop publishing—the skills you pick up will be rewarding you for decades to come.

Alternatively, there are two must-read introductory books on the subject:

• *The Non Designer's Design Book*—Robin WIlliams, Peachpit Press 1994. Packed with dos and don'ts, all illustrated with examples. Will have you cringing as you spot the flaws in the work you have done in the past.

• *The Layout Index*—Jim Krause, North Light Books 2001. Jim Krause has done layout work for McDonalds and Microsoft among others, and this book is over 300 pages of ideas and inspiration.

Reading these books won't make you an expert, any more than having an understanding of music theory will make you a composer. But they will help you avoid common traps, and the "backyard" tag that goes with amateurish layouts. And it might just be the reason that your ad is the one that parents consistently read first.

> **Long after you've forgotten the fact that you spent an extra $400 on a printer, you'll be enjoying the advantages of documents that look better than those of your competitors.**

Spend time on the bike

Armed with the tools you need to produce great brochures, and the knowledge you need to do it well, you then need to practice. The first couple of layouts will be the hardest you ever do. You'll swear at your computer as you wonder how to do X, or why Y keeps happening even though you don't want it to. But once you get past these hurdles, you can reuse your discoveries next time.

It won't be long before you'll be able to churn out designs easily and quickly (that's what your computer is for!)—the only difficulty will be choosing between them.

Get a good printer

You'll quickly discover that getting documents of any sort printed professionally is a very expensive exercise, making it a necessity to be able to print them yourself. But no matter how great your layout looks on the screen, if your printer is not up to the task, you'll get cheap looking results.

Again, you're purchasing what is really promotion infra-structure. You'll get what you pay for, and with possible new student enquiries at stake (which is your very livelihood!), it's worth buying the best you can afford. Long after you've forgotten the fact that you spent an extra $400 on a printer, you'll be enjoying the fact that all your documents look better than those of your competitors.

Just another unfair advantage, and you want as many as you can get.

> **The junk mail you receive mail is not just intrusive advertising.**
>
> **...it's a great chance to steal layout ideas from other people.**

Critically assess every ad you see

One of your best sources of inspiration and cautions will be other people's ads. Copy the things you like, analyze what it is that contributes to the things you don't. When your mailbox fills up with junk mail, you should actually be *happy*. For you, it's not just intrusive advertising—it's a great chance to steal layout ideas from other people. (I promise you, they are all stealing layout ideas from each other!)

Know your limitations

You may well get a great idea for an ad where a clarinet ties itself into a treble clef, while a statue of Weber looks on and shrugs its shoulders, superimposed over a smiling photo of you which transforms Escher-style into a passage of sixteenth notes. Very nice. But unless your PhotoShop skills are first rate, and you have LOTS of spare time, don't even think about it. The key to producing great looking advertisements is to know you are capable of technically, and to stay within those boundaries. You're trying to attract students, not win advertising artistic awards, and less is almost always more.

So by all means, upgrade your skills and equipment. But then work intelligently with what you've got—a solid idea executed well is always going to look better than a brilliant idea where your reach ended up exceeding your grasp.

Use quality stationery

If you want your letters and brochures to leave an impression that your studio is thriving, then you should use stationery that only a thriving studio would consider. The next time you are planning a letterbox drop, spend an extra couple of cents per page and use quality paper with a textured finish, tri-fold it and use a mock wax-seal to seal it. As you know from your own mailbox, most junk mail goes unread into the trash—your aim is to intrigue the recipient enough that they have to at least *open* it. (A seal is great for that!).

It will probably still end up in the trash, but not before a subtle message about the creativity and standards of your studio have been absorbed. If your letterbox drops show this level of care and artistry, what then of your teaching?

What's next?

No matter how good your advertisements look, one thing is certain. Most of the inquiries you then receive will be over the *phone*—which means that your voicemail message is a key ambassador for your studio.

The next section looks at how you can get the most out of your humble **answering machine**, with some simple techniques you can use to ensure that your message leaves a great impression.

Your voicemail message

First things first. If you don't have an answering machine of some sort, run, don't walk, and go get one. Nothing will kill an enquiry faster than a phone that rings with no answer. Unless you can guarantee to be home 24/7 to answer phone calls, you need to have something that will do it on your behalf—otherwise callers will simply move on to the next number in the Yellow Pages.

Simply having the machine is only part of the story though. When prospective students hear your recorded message, they will establish first impressions about both you and your studio. If that impression is not good, they're likely to just hang up, and your relationship with the student is terminated *even before you meet.*

It can take months of bad lessons to lose an existing student. But you can achieve the same unhappy outcome with a

> **If you spent less than an hour designing and recording your answering machine message, you weren't taking the task seriously enough.**

prospective student in less than ten seconds if your phone message is weak.

We'll look in a moment at some dos and don'ts for your voicemail message, but in the meantime, here's a simple test:

If you spent less than an hour designing and then recording your answering machine message, you weren't taking the task seriously enough.

Sound a little extreme?

Ask yourself this. If you were *hiring* someone to answer your studio's phone, what expectations would you have of their telephone manner? Remember, this person will be talking to potential students long before you get a chance to weave your magic at an interview, so they need to be friendly, polite, confident, clear, articulate and welcoming. Otherwise there's not going to be an interview in the first place.

Not only that, you should think carefully about *what* they say when they answer the phone. How would you react if you overheard your receptionist answer the phone like this?:

> "Hello. I don't really have time to listen to you at the moment. Tell me some way of getting in touch with you, and I'll get back to you when I don't have better things to do."

With that statement ringing in your ears, now think about your existing outgoing message. Does it sound like the following? (A lot of music teacher's do!):

> *"Hello, this is Sandy. I'm not able to take your call right now. Leave your name and number after the beep."*

Look at this message for a moment from the caller's point of view. There are plenty of problems, and they start with the first sentence:

> *"Hello, this is Sandy."*

You may well be Sandy, but if your studio is called "Happy Flutes Music School", then callers are going to be confused by a greeting that doesn't refer to that. With nothing else in the message that identifies you as providing music lessons, there will be some doubt as to whether or not it's actually the right number. At that point, a lot of people will simply hang up.

Even those who proceed regardless will be struck by the fact that the message sounds alarmingly like a *residence* phone message (rather than a business one), creating an impression of an amateur home based operation.

Even if your studio *is* home based — and most music teachers do work from home — if your phone number is also the *studio* phone number, then the message has to be for the studio too.

So instead of:

"Hello, this is Sandy."

Add on

"Hello, this Sandy, and the number for Happy Flutes Music Studio."

A lot of music teachers don't refer to their studio at all in their message, because the telephone line also doubles as a personal line and such a message feels inappropriate for family and friends who might call. You can't afford to be coy like this—teaching is your business, and your voicemail message needs to clearly confirm that. If a dual-function message like that still feels uncomfortable for you, then consider taking out a second phone line, dedicated to your studio.

The next part of the message is more difficult. Like all outgoing voicemail messages, you have to admit to not being available, and ask the caller to leave their details. But you can do so in such a way that makes not being available a virtue, rather than a nuisance, while also subtly telling them a thing or two about your studio.

So instead of

"I'm not able to take your call right now. Leave your name and number after the beep."

Consider

"I'm probably in the studio teaching at the moment. I'd love to chat with you though— leave your name and number, and I'll get back to you as soon as I can"

This leaves the caller with several important impressions:

1) That you are often busy teaching in the studio. So your studio must be a busy one. So you must be doing a good job.

2) That lessons at your studio are *not* interrupted by phone calls. Students get your undivided attention, while voicemail handles the distractions.

3) That you're friendly and outgoing. "I'd love to chat with you though" is much more welcoming than the more neutral "Leave your name and number".

4) Just in case they missed the name of your studio in the initial greeting, further reference to the studio in the second half of the message confirms that they have reached the right number

5) The fact that you have taken the trouble to refer twice to your studio in the message means that teaching is obviously no mere hobby for you. You are prepared to proudly state it at the gateway to your home.

Delivering the message with flair

Getting the text of the message right is not enough — most of the impression will be created by how you actually deliver it. You don't need to sound like a World Championship Wrestling announcer, but if your message is delivered in a flat monotone, then callers will picture flat, monotonous music lessons. It has to sparkle, it has to feel friendly and inviting...in short it has to sound like someone who should be working with kids.

Nobody likes listening to themselves on tape, but you *have* to preview the message before you let it represent your studio. If there is anything you are not happy with, then record it again. And again. And again. Experiment with different inflexions, with different speed of delivery. Try punching different words. It can take quite a while before you declare "That one! That's it" — but once you've produced a version you're happy with, it will represent you for a long time.

This might sound like overkill. It's not. Everything in your Lobby matters, and if your extra care results in just one extra student, your efforts will all have been worthwhile.

Don't memorize this piece

Before you push the "record outgoing message" on your machine, take a moment and write out exactly what it is that you're going to say. That way you can concentrate on delivery, rather than stumbling over trying to remember the words.

Making the message friendly

If you want your message to sound friendly as well as engaging, you should actually *smile* as you're delivering it. Truly. Forget that you're talking to a machine, and pretend you're addressing a cute six-year old instead. Your tone will soften, and your message will sound warmer and more inviting.

It's not just smoke and mirrors. Part of your job is that you *do* have to talk to cute six-year-olds anyway, and parents who listen to your message need to be able to imagine you relating to their child. Make it easy for them with a message that will speak volumes about your manner.

What's next?

Sooner or later, your advertisements are going to have to refer to your **qualifications**. But it's not the qualifications you have now that will help. It's the ones you don't have yet.

The next section looks at why you should be constantly upgrading, and what sorts of qualifications are most likely to excite parents.

The qualification edge

Whether you like it or not, one of the first things parents are likely to scan any ad for is *qualifications*. Not because qualifications necessarily make a better teacher, but because qualifications are the only objective assessment of your studio they have—a rock of stability in what is otherwise merely advertising copy.

As a result, you can claim all you like to run "Creative and child-centered lessons with expert tuition", but if you only have high school training in music, a parent who is genuinely interested in the "expert tuition" is going to go for the ad that mentions the teacher's postgraduate qualifications in music.

So while having a degree in music does not guarantee that parents will be interested, it certainly doesn't hurt your case any. Especially if your ad is the first they saw on the page that can make such a claim.

> **Most other music teachers will have exactly the same qualifications in ten years' time that they do now.**
>
> **What could *your* CV boast in 10 years?**

The need for qualifications doesn't mean that you have to stop your life for a decade while you go and pursue a Ph.D. in music. On the contrary – if you want to impress parents with your qualifications, you don't necessarily want *depth*.

You want *breadth*.

In other words, you want lots of qualifications. and you want the titles of the qualifications to tell the parents a thing or two about the great things they can expect in lessons. So a diploma in music technology means that you don't just *have* MIDI stuff in your studio, but that you actually know how to *use* it. If the parent reading your ad has a child who is interested in computers, your diploma in music technology is going to put you on a short list straight away.

It all helps differentiate you from the pack, and you can rest secure in the knowledge *that most other teachers will have exactly the same qualifications in ten years that they do now.* What could *your* CV boast in 10 years? How compelling could it be for prospective students?

Never mind ten years though—no matter where your qualifications are up to at the moment, there's a lot you can do in *this year* to address this issue. It's time to take the first small step to upgrading your skills again.

Upgrading your Qualifications

Don't pull that face at me. Upgrading your qualifications is not as hard as you think, and it doesn't have to involve a new four year degree. But quite independently of the work involved, fresh qualifications will repay you for many years to come—not just because they make your ads look better, but because of the new and exciting options they will bring to your studio. You're not just doing these courses to pick up certificates. You're also developing brand new skills. So a basic sound engineering and recording course isn't just one more qualification for your list. It could mean that your studio could actually produce its *own* recordings.

Which is then something you can mention in its own right:

"Every child produces their own CD, capturing forever their progress through the studio recording label"

No matter what your current level of musical schooling, it's always possible to take new courses. A cartooning course for reminders on their page that they can't ignore. A public speaking course so that you don't just introduce student recitals, you leave parents and students fired up for the year that's ahead. A desktop publishing course so you can produce compelling studio newsletters and brochures. A diploma in child psychology, specializing in motivating children.

In fact, every year, your advertising should be able to refer to qualifications that you did not possess the year before. In the music teaching world, old dogs who ignore new tricks will in turn be ignored by prospective students in favour of other teachers who seem to be offering more.

In short, if you want your phone to ring, keep upgrading your skills.

Quite apart from the extra listings in your ads, imagine what a decade of such regular professional development would actually do for your teaching?

Where to start

Become a course-brochures junkie. Call every local educational institution that offers course for adults, and ask for their course outlines — sensing a potential student themselves, most will be delighted to oblige. You'll use the brochures partly so you know what you would be in for, but mostly to help inspire you as to what's possible in the first place.

Keep an open mind, and be slow to rule out courses. While there will obviously be some that will be of no use whatsoever to your teaching (e.g. beekeeping for beginners), when you read through the brochure with your teaching hat on, you'll be amazed at how many have applications in music lessons. Daydream a little, imagine what's possible, then choose the course that seems to provide the most options.

Consider highlighting your non-musical qualifications

What I'm about to propose comes as a surprise to most music teachers.

The qualifications you highlight don't all have to be about music to help you stand out from the crowd. In fact, qualifications in just about *any* of the interests you have outside music can be an asset.

Let's take an extreme example. An advanced certificate in Stage Magic might sound like something that you'd keep to yourself, but it actually tells parents that your lessons are likely to be unpredictable and fun, and that you'll probably be able to make their child laugh. So if you have such a certificate, you should mention it, no matter how irrelevant to music it may seem.

A Level 2 Tennis Coaching certificate tells parents that there is more to you than just treble clefs and accidentals. And that you have experience with working with kids that goes beyond the studio walls.

All you want is for that initial phone call to take place, and if it came about simply because the parent was intrigued to read that just like their daughter, you have a chess rating of over 1900, then so be it.

Remember, parents aren't just looking for someone who knows about scales and arpeggios. They want someone who can *connect* with their child, and one of your extra qualifications might just be the unfair advantage you need.

> **Remember, parents aren't just looking for someone who knows about scales and arpeggios.**
>
> **They want someone who can *connect* with their child.**

What's next?

Now the fun really starts. Having confronted your **past promotion efforts**, constructed your **Future Teaching Schedule**, adopted a **more appropriate fee** for services, acquired the **desktop publishing tools** you need, polished your **voicemail message** and planned the first of a series of **qualification upgrades**, it's time to start thinking about the promotion campaign itself.

The second half of this book is filled with more campaign ideas than you could ever use, all with one thing in mind:

Making your Future Teaching Schedule — and all the benefits that come with that — a reality.

Campaign Elements

A barrel full of **promotion ideas** for your studio

Yellow Pages • The local factor • Reciprocated business cards • Become a media expert • Discounts for referrals • Combine forces with other teachers • Advertise a scholarship • Free lessons in the holidays • Teacher exchange program • Target a niche • Become involved in your local schools • Strategic Partnerships • Make use of your car • Reciprocal Promotions • Keep local media informed about student successes • Create and sell a resource • Organize a practice-a-thon • Advertise student concerts • Letterbox drop • Become active in your local MTA • Offer free lessons as a raffle prize • Give a free seminar • Make the pie bigger • Create a competitions •

Yellow Pages Advertising

There is no single more effective piece of paid advertising than a well designed Yellow Pages ad. When parents are considering music lessons for their child, Yellow Pages will often be the first place they will look—in fact for many parents, it's the *only* place they look.

> **When calls go to other teachers instead of you, it's not always because they are better teachers.**
>
> **It's often simply because their ad was big enough to be noticed.**

You want to make sure that when they do, your name is there, and that it stands out from the pack.

For this reason, you should not only ensure that you are listed, *but that you have taken out the biggest ad you can afford.* (In fact, it should be bigger than you think you can afford—more on this in a moment)

Before you write off this idea as being too expensive, you should do so with a full understanding of what *not* doing it might be costing you.

The power of a big ad

1) More likely to be noticed

Yellow Pages themselves will have all the statistics on how users search through listings, but all the studies confirm that it's the big ads that get the lion's share of the attention. When calls go to other teachers instead of you, it's not always because they are better teachers. It's often just because their ad was big enough to be noticed.

If you find this hard to believe, take note of your own behavior the next time you use Yellow Pages. Who did you call? Was it one of the two line listings at the end of the section? Or was it one of the big display ads that you noticed first?

In fact, how many of the non-display ads did you even *see?*

2) Creates an impression of a thriving studio

The assumption is that if you have one of the bigger ads, you must be one of the more successful studios in town. And if you're one of the more successful studios, then you must be one of the better teachers. Not necessarily true of course, but it's the perception that's going to cause your phone to ring.

It goes back to the principle that's central to promoting your studio — if you want a big studio with a full waiting list, *you have to appear like a big studio with a full waiting list.* It becomes a self-fulfilling prophecy, and you'll quickly forget the pain of the cost of the ad once the calls start to come in.

> **The more information parents have available, the more real your studio will seem—and the more likely they will be to call you in the first place.**

3) More physical space to display your message

Instead of having to limit yourself to simply your studio name and phone number, you can include a teaching philosophy, a link to your studio website, details about your facilities, or even a photo. It means that your studio will have substance, while the shorter listings of other teachers will simply be numbers and names in the crowd. The more information parents have available, the more real your studio will seem — and the more likely they will be to call you in the first place.

4) Raises your profile among your colleagues.

When each new Yellow Pages edition comes out, the first thing other music teachers in your town will do is check their own ad. But their ad won't be the only ad they notice. They'll notice the ads of close colleagues — and they'll also notice the bigger ads.

This can mean that if a teacher of another instrument is asked to recommend someone who teaches *your* instrument, your name will probably leap to mind. Again, their assumption will be that because you have a big ad, your studio is doing well—so you must be doing something right.

5) Raises your profile among retailers of complementary products.

In many Yellow Pages listings, "music teachers" are displayed near the "music stores" listings—which means that all the local music stores probably saw your ad when they checked out their own ad. Thanks to your large ad, the next time they are asked to name a teacher of your instrument, your name is likely to come up.

> If you spend money on an ad, you're not saying goodbye to that money —it should actually pay for itself, and then bring in extra on top of that.

The benefits to these stores knowing about your studio goes well beyond the fact that they might recommend you. As we'll see, many of these stores are actually also potential strategic partners, and your big ad will ensure that by the time you're pitching a joint-marketing idea to them, they already know about you (There's not a lot of value for them creating a partnership with a studio nobody has ever heard of!).

So how much should you spend?

Depending on where you live, big display ads in Yellow Pages can be very expensive, but an ad is not like buying a car, or television set. If you spend money on an ad, you're not saying goodbye to that money—it should actually pay for itself, and then bring in extra on top of that. In other words, you have to reframe your thinking so that you regard it as an investment, not as an expense. The reality is—perversely it might seem—that *not* spending the extra will actually *cost* you money. So if you expect an ad to do big things for you, then you need to be prepared to upsize the ad. Before you look at booking yourself a commercial in the half time break of the SuperBowl though, you need to make some basic calculations about what your investment should be.

The first thing you should do is talk to some other music teachers with equivalent or bigger ads, and ask how many enquiries those ads produce each year. Based on your own knowledge of your ability to convert enquiries to new students, you can then work out how many new students each year that number of enquiries should produce.

> **If you simply have a two line listing, *your studio will be treated like all the other two line listings.***
>
> **In other words, you'll never be noticed in the first place.**

The logic then is to assume that a quarter of all the new students that the ad produces will go towards covering the cost of the ad itself. (This allows you to be wrong in your estimates by a factor of four, and still break even).

So a simple calculation you can perform is:

Number of estimated new students the ad will produce, divided by four, and multiplied by your annual income from one student.

That's your figure for the display ad. Take a deep breath, and look at it.

That number is probably much higher than you ever would have contemplated spending on advertising otherwise. Be brave though — the results can be spectacular.

Are there any guarantees?

No. As for all forms of advertising, there is an element of risk. But there is one certainty — if you simply have a two line listing, then your studio will be treated like all the other two line listings by potential students.

In other words, you'll never be noticed in the first place.

Learn from the experiences of others

You're not the only business who will be wrestling with how much to spend on Yellow Pages, and wondering just how effective a bigger (or color) ad might be.

If you're still seeking reassurance and advice, talk to other businesses, and they don't have to be at all music related. Pick some ads that are the same size as the ads you are considering for your own studio, and give the businesses that placed the ad a quick call. Let them know that you're a first time display advertiser, and just wondering what their experience has been with the whole adventure.

Most businesses will be more than happy to spend a minute or so giving you their version of events. After you've talked to a dozen or so, you'll have a better understanding of what to expect, and will probably be feeling more relaxed about your investment.

In most cases, they will confirm what the Yellow Pages reps will tell you anyway — if you have a large ad, your phone is going to ring.

Triple check the copy

You're stuck with this ad for a whole year, with no way of correcting errors. When they send you proof copy, read it VERY carefully — in fact, better still, give it to a couple of other people to read. A simple misspelling will leave you looking unprofessional, while a missed digit in a phone number can mean that you cannot be contacted in the first place.

One quick example — a couple of years ago a charter bus company here in my home town advertised "Good rates on school *executions*". I'm pretty sure they meant "excursions", but for 365 days it had people wondering just how tough discipline is in

Australian schools. You don't want your ad appearing on Jay Leno. (Actually, then again...it would be great publicity...)

Keep your ad fresh

Don't fall into the trap of placing the same ad every year — your ad should evolve as your studio does. This is partly so you can experiment with different sizes and copy, allowing you to gradually fine tune your approach.

But it's mostly so that other music teachers and music related business can see that there's no moss gathering on even this most mundane aspect of your studio. The fact that your ad is always fresh and different will suggest that your lessons are creative and always under review too.

Consider professional help with layout

Part of your studio promotion strategy should be developing your desktop publishing skills, but this is one ad that you definitely cannot afford to have an amateur stamp on.

We've all skipped over ads just because they *look* bad — if you have to spend a few hundred extra to ensure your ad looks as professional as your studio is, then it's worth every cent. Remember, at the instant that the student is looking at your ad for the first time, the design and layout of the ad itself constitutes a huge percentage of your Lobby. In fact for someone who hasn't actually read the copy yet, and therefore might know nothing about you, design and layout is 100% of your Lobby!

If the cost frightens you, remember that if just *one* student comes aboard because they were impressed by the fact that your ad looked great, then your extra outlay will have covered itself very quickly.

No matter how much we are counselled not to judge books by their cover, we all still do. And if creating a great cover means getting some extra help, then so be it.

The power of walking distance

No matter how well credentialed your studio may be, no matter how state-of-the-art your facilities, for many parents the choice of a music teacher comes down to one thing:

"Is the studio *nearby*?"

The answer to this question will then answer dozens of others for them. And for busy parents, the issue of proximity will be of much greater interest than whether or not you topped your year in musicology:

> **This is no time to be wasting copy on your repertoire or teaching philosophies.**
>
> **Simply ensure that these posters feature your address—and the fact that it's within walking distance—very prominently.**

"How long will I have to spend driving to and from the lesson each week? Can my child ride a bike, or even walk? Is it near the playing fields where my other child has soccer practice? Can I take care of delivering them both in one round trip? How far from the local shops is it? Do I have time to pick up a few groceries before the lesson ends?"

As any parent with school age kids knows, logistics are an important consideration before committing to any activity. Time is at a premium in a week that is filled to bursting with other activities, and however trivial you may regard location as being, *it will sometimes be the reason parents call in the first place.*

You want to ensure that parents who are nearby know about your studio, and that it's just around the corner. The trick here is not in what advertising technique you choose — it's in the focus of the message.

Shop windows

A simple way to target parents who are concerned about the "local" issue is to put posters in local shop windows, and to ensure that those posters feature your address—and the fact that it's walking distance—very prominently. This is no time to be wasting copy on your repertoire or teaching philosophies. Catch their eye with the "`Expert flute lessons - 2 min walk from this poster`" notice.

For many busy parents, that's all they need to hear.

Special mailout campaign

The chapter on mailout tactics recommends that you limit the area of circulation to those households that are within a fifteen minute walk of your studio, ensuring that you'll be perceived as being "nearby". But if you really want to highlight the sheer convenience of having lessons at your studio, you should consider a second mailout—a special one that will only be going to households that are within a *five* minute walk of where you teach.

The message on this mailout can be different from the wider mailout—because these people are so close, it can read almost as one neighbor to another. Instead of just giving street names, you can be a little friendlier, mentioning landmarks that most of your neighbors will know:

> "I'm just across the road from Dr. Henderson's vet practice"

> "My studio is that blue house behind the bus stop on Maple Drive"

If you teach an instrument that is a little louder, such as piano or trumpet, you can even refer to the fact that the person reading your ad has probably *heard* your studio in action, perhaps without realizing quite what it was. Your letter can then explain the source of the music, and then extend an invitation to find out about your studio for themselves:

"If you've ever walked down Maple Drive in the afternoon, you've probably heard piano playing floating from the blue house.

That's not a recording—it's *kids*. School children from all over this neighborhood learning to play Mozart. I'd love to help your kid play too—drop by any afternoon at 6:15, and I'll take you on a tour of what's possible."

Sign on your house

Depending on where you live, you could well have hundreds of different people walking past your home each day, many of whom will live nearby. It's not as though putting up a sign will suddenly make them all want music lessons, but it will ensure that those who are interested will know just how conveniently located you are.

As for all your display advertising, the quality of the sign is important. It's not enough to paint a notice on some butcher's paper—spend a little extra and have a professional signwriter custom build something for you. A cheap looking sign will not only fail to attract students, it might actively hurt your cause.

> **A cheap looking sign will not only fail to attract students, it might actively hurt your cause.**

Before you do anything though, you'll need to check council regulations about such advertisements—in some cities business signage is not permitted in residential areas. (In fact, some councils won't like the fact that you are running a business from a residence in the first place, so your billboard on the lawn might attract attention that you don't want)

Include maps and facts

Where space permits, all your advertisements should include a map of some sort. Make sure it includes surrounding streets, so that visitors can not only see your studio, but can relate its location to their own home. (Teachers in the US who create a free PracticeSpot web advertisement for their studio will have a map automatically generated once they input their address—see p 218 for more details)

You should also mark schools and shops clearly on the map, reinforcing the message that your studio is right next door to the places the parents most commonly need to visit. If you have the information handy, it might also be worth including some relevant distance facts:

- `1.5 km from` **`CenterTown Plaza`**

- `Five minute walk from` **`CenterTown High School`**

- `2 blocks east from` **`CenterTown Day-care Center`**

In this way, parents are not only able to relate your studio to their own homes, but to the other activities that occupy their week—which is an effective way of having them picture it as part of their week in the first place.

Reciprocated Business Cards

On the front counters of many small businesses you will find business cards for other (usually non-competing) enterprises. So when you pop in to your local baker, you might find on their front counter business cards for locksmiths, interior decorators, math tuition services or auto-repair yards.

Why? Because these locksmiths, interior decorators, math tutors and mechanics know that plenty of their potential customers *also buy bread*—and so they set up reciprocating business cards. The baker's card will appear on the front counter of all those businesses, in return for those businesses being able to leave their card on the baker's front counter. Customers waiting for their order to be completed often idly glance at the cards on the counter-top, and if they currently happen to be looking for a math tutor for their child, they'll probably take the relevant card.

Well, guess what. Some of these bread-buying customers will have been thinking about *music lessons* for their child too. Which is why you need to make sure that your card is there—being in the right place at the right time.

> **Customers waiting for their order to be completed often idly glance at business cards on the counter-top.**
>
> **You want to make sure your card is in the right place at the right time.**

Making it worth their while

So what can you offer those businesses in return? You can actually offer much more than mere reciprocation. Your customers don't just spend thirty seconds near displayed business cards while their transactions are processed. Your customers spend thirty *minutes* waiting in your studio, listening to their child play, and are highly likely to read just about anything that is within eyeshot. Just as we all do when we're stuck waiting in doctor's waiting rooms.

By the end of the semester, they probably will have memorized the contents of every poster, business card and brochure that you have lying about.

So while you can't offer the advantage of having hundreds of different clients seeing the cards each week, you *can* offer repeated exposure in a way that the baker probably can't. If you have a card in your studio for "Henderson's Glass Repair", by the end of the year, "Henderson's" will spring to mind for all your students the next time they hit a ball through a window. It might only bring Henderson's one job per year from you. And your business card on Henderson's front counter might only bring you one new student enquiry. But that's one glass repair

> **This tactic might only bring you one new enquiry each year.**
>
> **But that's one more than you would have got otherwise.**

job for Hendersons, and one enquiry more for you than would have taken place otherwise — it's a win-win.

To help stack the numbers in your favour, don't just chat with a Glass Repairer though. You want your card in a dozen different small businesses.

And the price you pay for all this? Printing costs of the business card (which you could actually do yourself in any case), and loss of some table or pinboard space in your studio.

What if they say no?

So be it. Ask someone else. The Yellow Pages are packed with opportunities, and even if you had to approach two hundred small businesses to get the dozen that say "yes", it's well worth your time.

You can make a "yes" much more likely if:

a) If you already are a known customer to that business. If you buy your Chinese Takeaway from the same restaurant every week, that takeaway will have much more reason to trust you than a business that you just cold call. Take ten minutes and make a list of the places you regularly shop, and the services you regularly use—those should definitely be your starting point.

> **The added bonus is that a lot of these business owners are not just business owners...**
>
> **...a lot of them are parents too.**

b) **You don't waste any more of their time than is absolutely necessary.** Have cards ready with you, and be ready to take away theirs. Be brief, friendly, businesslike, and interested in what they have to say.

c) **You offer the opportunity to review the arrangement in a few months**, to give them a chance to gracefully exit if it doesn't prove useful.

d) That in the meantime, **their business card will be the ONLY card for that line of business.** So if you are approaching "Beautiful Snips Hair Salon", you would only be then approaching "Cindy's Hair Boutique" if "Beautiful Snips" is not interested. In other words, if they say yes, the arrangement is exclusive. This not only gives added value to the arrangement, but gently reminds "Beautiful Snips" that if they say "no", your clients might be looking at "Cindy's" card every week instead.

e) **That you genuinely don't mind if they say "no".** Don't push, just thank them for their time. People are much more likely to say "yes" if you don't sound as though being able to pay for your sister's kidney transplant depends on the outcome.

So where do you start with all this? Carry a notepad with you for a couple of weeks while you go about your regular shopping. Start building a list of businesses to target—*with a particular focus on those businesses that already have business cards of others on display.* That way you only have to sell yourself, because they are obviously already receptive to the idea.

Then get your cards designed and printed, rehearse your brief intro about yourself and the possibility of reciprocal business cards, and go ring some bells at some counters.

Consider a call-for-replacements scheme

A call-for-replacements agreement simply means that should visitors to your studio have taken all the cards for a particular business, *you will call that business to let them know that you need more* – and in the same circumstances, they would make a similar call to you.

Not only does this ensure that there is a constant supply of cards, it also provides valuable tracking information for both your studio and their business. You'll know which businesses are providing regular nibbles for you, helping you place future cards more effectively. And they'll know that their cards are being seen.

Fringe benefits

The added bonus to a reciprocated business card placement is that these business owners are not just business owners. A lot of them are parents too...meaning that if your approach was professional, friendly and was not an imposition, they'll know your name in the event that their own kids want music lessons.

As with so many other promotion tactics, you never know where the ripples may end up once the stone is cast. And it should be clear even this early in the book that you should be planning on casting many, many stones.

Set yourself a target

To help put wind in your sails, set a number of businesses to approach, and keep on ringing bells at desks until you've met that quota. Don't worry too much about whether or not they are saying "yes" or not, just concentrate on making the approaches in the first place.

> **A year of this, and your card will be representing your studio in dozens of places that it would never have otherwise.**

If only 10% of businesses say "yes" (and that might not be far off the mark), than that's going to make for a modest campaign if you only approach 10 different businesses in the first place.

But if you approach *200* businesses, then you're likely to end up with 20 that are interested. That's 20 places that have a little portable advertisement for your teaching studio.

Where are earth are you going to find the time to approach 200 businesses? Do it a bit at a time. Set aside one day each fortnight on which you'll approach 10 businesses — shouldn't take you much more than an hour each time. A year of this, and you will have made contact with 260 other businesses, and your card will be representing your studio in dozens of places that it would never have otherwise.

Keep track of where your cards are

To save yourself the embarrassment of approaching the same business more than once, keep records of who you approach, together with what the outcome was. A quick analysis of such records will also then start to paint you a profile of which business types are the most promising for future contact, helping save you time.

Become a media expert

One of the best ways to become the best known music teacher in town…is to become the best known music teacher in town. Which means its time to start making use of the one institution that commands everyone's attention.

The Media.

The New York Times probably won't run the article you put together, but your local Midville Chronicle just might. And a lot of parents who live near your studio browse through papers like that while they munch on their cornflakes.

When end-of-year concerts start to draw near, prepare a series of short articles helping music students with their preparation, and volunteer them to your local paper. Practice techniques, coping with nerves, things to do (or not to do), how parents can help…there's plenty of potential material.

Make sure that you are armed with statistics on how many music students there are in the distribution area — you have to help the newspaper see how this will be of benefit to them too. (It's usually an attractive figure!). And you won't be expecting payment for your work.

Your local radio station might also be interested in having you in to talk about getting ready for the Big Day. It's not as though you are talking about Sumerian Agricultural Tools. Music lessons are a big part of lots of families' lives, and there are plenty of producers who would be happy to consider a brief spot that targeted such an everyday issue. Send them an email outlining what you are planning to chat about, see what they say.

> **The New York Times probably won't run the article you put together, but your local Midville Chronicle just might.**
>
> **And a lot of parents who live near your studio browse through papers like that while they munch on their cornflakes.**

The point is, you won't know unless you ask. If they say no, then so be it.

And if they say yes, *you are suddenly the local expert on learning a musical instrument.* Don't be surprised if some enquiries follow.

Suggest topics that may interest local media

Before you shoot off your interview proposal, you need to ensure that it's going to prove interesting to potential listeners/ viewers/readers. Just because you are an expert on minimizing part-crossing in Plagal Cadences doesn't mean that Letterman wants to talk to you about it.

Look at the topic from the point of view of parents or students. Will it interest them enough to stop them from leaving the room for a couple of minutes? With parents investing so much time and money in music lessons, if your segment sounds like it will help them in some way, they'll pay attention.

Some ideas:
- When your child won't practice
- Things parents considering music lessons should know
- 10 signs that your child might be ready for music lessons
- 10 signs that your child might be gifted musically
- How to help your child get the most out of their music lessons
- How to help your child choose the right instrument/ teacher
- 10 hidden benefits of having music lessons
- How to help your child cope with pre-concert nerves

You'll have no trouble thinking of your own, although if you get stuck, there is plenty of inspiration at the official practicespot press website at **www.practicespot.com**.

What if they won't talk to you/won't run your story?

Don't give up. There are plenty of other newspapers, magazines, radio stations and television stations around, and you need to be ready for the fact that many of them — even most of them — might say no. But if just *one* says "Yes — would Wednesday at 4:12 pm suit?", just consider how much it would have cost to actually *buy* that many column inches, or that six minute slice of radio air time.

Whatever happens, if you are on the receiving end of a rejection, you certainly shouldn't try to change the editor's/producer's mind. All that will do is guarantee that they will ignore you completely the next time.

So if the mail brings bad news, simply throw the rejections in the bin, and get on with the next submission. The potential reward is too big to ignore, and after you've had one acceptance, it's much easier to get a second.

> **...if they say yes, *you are suddenly the local expert on learning a musical instrument.***
>
> **Don't be surprised if some enquiries follow.**

Consider out-of-area publications too

Writing for a magazine or newspaper interstate won't help you attract students directly, but it will help give you credibility. The readers of Parenting Monthly Magazine might all live too far away to consider lessons with you, but the very fact that they are publishing your thoughts on music teaching means that you can proudly state in your ads:

As featured in Parenting Monthly Magazine

Just another reason for prospective students to call you instead of the opposition — or at least for them to be curious enough to want to find out more.

MASTERCLASS: Staying motivated

This book provides plenty of ideas for promoting your studio, but ideas alone are not going to transform anything. You have to actually make those ideas *happen*.

The problem is that effective promotion is not just a wind-up-and-forget exercise—it's an ongoing commitment, and will require a significant investment of time. To maintain the levels of creativity and enterprise required to consistently enhance your studio's profile is hard work, and you're not always going to feel like it.

> **Effective promotion is not just a wind-up-and-forget exercise.**
>
> **It's an ongoing commitment, and will require a significant investment of time.**

So how will you cope when your batteries are running low, and it all feels like too much? There are some simple things you can do to help you stay the course.

Daily diary of "What steps did I take today?"

To help keep you focused on the target, you should maintain a **daily log** of your promotion accomplishments.

Purchase an appointment book—one that has plenty of blank lines for each day of the year. At the end of each day, record all the steps you took on that day towards building your studio. Posters designed, phone calls made, advertising copy written, ads of others that you've analyzed, local businesses approached, words written on your article for the local paper, letter drafted to parents about discounts for referrals—anything and everything.

It doesn't just have to be completed steps that you record. You might be in the middle of preparing a free seminar for prospective students, and have spent an hour working on the outline. In that case, you record:

```
• Spent an hour working on the outline for the
  seminar.
```

The diary will help motivate you in two ways.

First of all, it will provide a running record of all the promotion work you do complete, helping you feel a sense of accomplishment as each task is added to the list.

But most importantly, the fact that you have to record *something* each day will mean that you will want to ensure that there was something to record. Having to write in "Nothing today" is an awful feeling, and you'll usually find that you'll take a step of some sort—no matter how small— just so you don't have to leave the day blank.

> **The fact that you have to record *something* each day will mean that you will want to ensure that there was actually something to record.**

In that way, your daily log becomes like a person who is gently checking up on you. *"What did you do today to help make your future teaching schedule a reality?"* it will ask, and it will stare at you expectantly.

You'll be amazed at how hard it is to have to admit "Um....nothing, actually".

You'll also be amazed at how these small daily tasks add up. In three months, you will have recorded more than *ninety* of them, and if your phone is suddenly ringing a lot more than it used to, you won't need to wonder why.

This starts today. What have you done? At the very least, you can say that you spent time reading this book. ☺

Calculate the change in income

It's not tough arithmetic. Simply take a moment to work out what you currently earn in a year from your existing teaching schedule, and then perform the same calculation for your Future Teaching Schedule (see p 40). Be sure to add a few dollars per lesson in the process (Remember, once your studio has a waiting list, you're in a strong position to put up your fees).

> **An additional 35 students in your schedule would see you earn *a quarter of a million dollars* more in the next 10 years than you would have otherwise.**

The difference between the two annual figures should be quite impressive, but that's not the real story. You're not just planning on having a full studio for only 12 months.

You need to multiply the difference between the two incomes by *ten*, which will show you what impact your new schedule would have over a decade of teaching.

One quick illustration. Assuming a lesson fee of $18, if you were to have an additional 35 students in your schedule, you will earn *a quarter of a million dollars* more in the next 10 years than you would have otherwise.

What will you do with that extra income? I'm sure you'll have some good ideas. And the next time you feel like giving up on promotion, remind yourself that the penalty for quitting this particular race is $250,000. It's probably all you need to know.

Chart the growth in enquiries

To complement the daily recording of the steps you take towards promoting your studio, you should also keep track of *enquiries* as they come in. Find yourself a big "Year at a Glance" calendar, and put a small green spot under the appropriate date as prospective students call.

Alternatively, if you have set up one of PracticeSpot's free studio management websites for yourself (See p 226 for more information), you can track all enquiries through your Enquiry Manager. Either way, you want to be able to quickly and easily record enquiries as the phone rings.

Don't be discouraged if things are quiet at first. They're *supposed* to be quiet at first—all your creative promotion work will take time to have an impact.

But when the phone does start to ring, you'll be able to record the extra enquiries on your calendar, helping you see what a difference your existing efforts have made, and reminding you that additional efforts in the future will be worthwhile too.

In other words, you'll be able to see confirmation that all your work has *worked*.

Keep referring back to this book regularly

This book has plenty of options to get you started again if your engine stalls—even if you feel that you have carefully read every idea, it's worth taking the time to visit the ideas again every few months. You'll notice some options that you may have overlooked the first time, and others that you had originally dismissed as being impossible, but that now feel achievable.

There are also over a thousand pages of free information at the PracticeSpot website at www.practicespot.com, there are teacher newsgroups to participate in, and fellow teachers at your Local MTA who you can bounce ideas off, and be encouraged by.

In short, you're not alone. (You're also more than welcome to send me an email at philipj@practicespot.com)

Discounts for referrals

No matter how much time you spend polishing the copy for your yellow pages ad, or dropping leaflets in letterboxes, nothing beats word-of-mouth. To have a friend recommend a service is a trusted source indeed, and we've all purchased things in the past because friends have sworn by the product.

Many teachers are reluctant to embrace a discount-for-referrals scheme, feeling it smacks of desperation somehow, and will leave a bad taste in parents' mouths. It doesn't have to—but you do need to be careful about how you float such a proposal to them.

The best way to start it all is with a friendly note to parents.

> **To have a friend recommend a service is a trusted source indeed...**
>
> **...the best way to start it all is with a friendly note to parents.**

"*Dear Parents*

As you probably know, I am looking once again at expanding the studio, but am looking for word of mouth as the main trigger for interviews. (That way I can spend less time thinking about advertising and more time thinking about teaching!)

Such referrals are enormously useful to me—not just because they create enquiries, but because the enquiries tend to be warm from the outset rather than neutral. They've already heard good things about the studio, and it makes the interview an absolute joy.

As a thank you for referrals, this year I will be offering either a:

- $15 discount on fees **or**
- a large signed poster of me ☺

for any parent whose referral leads to an interview. (Your choice, but unless you strongly object to such acknowledgement of your efforts, I am encouraging you to opt for the discount.)

This would apply for *each* referral, so four interviews would result in a $60 deduction from your account.

I recognize that referrals would come about independently of whether or not there was a discount—but the fee reduction is there anyway as a genuine sign of appreciation. I trust your judgment about people you refer to me, and it makes my job much easier.

Referred students can set up an interview either by calling me, or emailing me through the studio website.

Best wishes etc."

The logic behind the poster

The "poster" offer isn't just there to lighten things up. Nobody is going to want a signed poster of you, but it does provide subtle recognition that some parents may be uncomfortable with the idea of accepting a discount for a referral. It also provides a gentle way of reminding parents that you're not "purchasing" referrals, but are simply expressing your gratitude for referrals that would have happened anyway.

Be generous with discounts

The discounts offered in the sample letter above may seem

over the top—after all, if one family's referrals result in 10 new interviews, they get a whopping $150 discount on their fees. But this is dwarfed by the additional income you would receive if only one of those students signs up. A new student can be worth thousands of dollars over several years, making the original incentive of $15 for the interview feel somewhat insignificant.

Alternatives incentives

If offering discount incentives feels a little mercenary, you might want to offer extra free music lessons instead. It's an acknowledgement of your appreciation that provides a similar benefit to your student, but doesn't create a direct association between referrals and a dollar value.

Another possibility is to set up a "Free Music Books" scheme—the deal being that you will supply for free all the required music books for any student who arranges a certain number of referrals. You can set this at several tiers:

Bronze: Next book is free (for 1 referral)
Silver: Next two books are free (For 3 referrals)
Gold: All books are free for the next two years (For 10 referrals)

Make it easy for them

Ensure that you have plenty of propaganda material readily available—brochures, fliers, together with your studio website address—so that there are tangible representations of your studio at hand. Parents won't all choose to make use of it, but the point is that it's there if they have further questions.

You should also be up front and enthusiastic about the scheme itself. Don't be apologetic or meek—all that will do is make the parents feel uncomfortable. Be candid with them about your goal of growing the studio, and genuine in your appreciation of their efforts and interest.

Consider a sunset clause

If your parent body is enthusiastic, and your incentives are appealing, a referral program can sometimes actually get out of hand. After all, if each of your students were to organize three referrals each, it doesn't take long before you simply wouldn't have space in your schedule any more. Once that happens, further referrals won't mean additional students for you—all it means is additional income lost through honoring the discounts.

> **If all of your students were to organize three referrals each, it doesn't take long before you simply wouldn't have space in your schedule any more.**

When you start the scheme, be clear about the conditions under which it can *end*. You can either specify a date, or simply indicate that the scheme can end at *any time* without notice.

Thank them and follow up

Once the interview from a referral is complete, make a point of phoning the parent to thank them for their efforts. While the events of the interview itself are confidential, if you feel it's warranted, there's nothing wrong with making a point of enthusing about the interviewee—after all, they are likely to be friends of the parent you are talking to, and they will be hoping that you were impressed by them too.

Your enthusiasm is then likely to be relayed back to the interviewee, helping things get off to a positive start should lessons commence. (And in fact helping them to decide that the lessons should commence in the first place)

Combine forces with other teachers

One great way to be able to cope with the cost of a large ad is to create a *group* of teachers. The group then shares both the ad, and all associated expenses. In this way, six teachers can co-operate to ensure that a commanding $3,000 ad only costs each participant $500.

So how does it work? The secret is ensuring that the members of the group *complement*, rather than *compete* with each other. So your ad could be for "Boydtown Music Tuition", but the six listed teachers might consist of flute, piano, oboe, clarinet, trumpet and voice, each with a separate listed number. Prospective students are much more likely to notice this ad than the smaller ad you would have done by yourself, and then they call the relevant teacher.

> **It's a powerful example of the whole being greater than the sum of its parts.**
>
> **You'll end up with an ad that will completely overshadow most of your competitors.**

Because of the complementary nature of the services on offer, sharing the ad like this *doesn't* mean that you have to share students. If you're the only oboe teacher in the group, then 100% of the parents who call "Boydtown Music Tuition" looking for oboe lessons will talk to you. And you'll have an advantage over the other oboe teachers, because they will be limited to whatever advertising they could afford by themselves. The advertisement for your group will overshadow your competitors'advertisements in a way that advertising by yourself never could have.

Each of the studios can retain their own autonomy—apart from co-operation on the ad itself, there is no need for any further official association between group members. Alternatively, the group might elect to take things further still, and create a business that reflects the association, perhaps even co-operating in a similar fashion on a centralized premises of some sort. But the point is, it doesn't *have* to be that grand. Even if all the group did was meet once a year to discuss next year's ad, the mechanics of the idea work just fine.

Combining with same-instrument colleagues

This technique is also possible for teachers who all teach the same instrument, but you will need to introduce some additional way of differentiating between the studios. For example, you could ensure that all members of the group were from different parts of the city. Or that different members of the group specialize in different styles, or different levels of proficiency, or different ages. Again, you don't end up losing prospective students to other group members, because all the students who are interested in your niche will call you, and only you.

Float the idea at your next MTA meeting—be clear on the structure, limitations and

> ...you don't end up losing prospective students to other group members...
>
> ...because the students who are interested in your niche will end up calling you, and only you.

benefits of the proposal, and let people know that if they are interested, they should contact you. Make sure you're already armed with some figures and examples of what's possible. It's much easier to excite fellow teachers about combining forces if they can actually see it in action.

Advertise a scholarship

Most studios don't offer scholarships—which is exactly why you should be considering one for *your* studio. The idea is that you would offer a year of free lessons to the most outstanding applicant, and handled intelligently, the whole scheme can create an enormous buzz among music students in your area.

Ideally, the candidates should be assessed in an audition by a panel of your trusted colleagues—*a panel which you would be merely a member of.* In other words, you don't have the deciding vote. This is to help create a perception of legitimacy for the verdict, and also to allow you to look students who *didn't* get it in the eye. They are less likely to feel betrayed by you if there exists the possibility that you may have even been overruled in your own wishes. (This is particularly important if your existing students are applying for the scholarship—you can stress to them that the final decision is not up to you, so they can't take anything personally!)

> **Many teachers are reluctant to "give away" a place like this in their studio.**
>
> **But the very existence of a scholarship is likely to bring plenty of fresh conventional enquiries to your studio.**

The hidden advantages

Many teachers are reluctant to "give away" a place like this in their studio, but the very existence of the scholarship is likely to bring plenty of fresh conventional enquiries to your studio. Partly because it creates the impression that your studio must not only be doing well (Wow! They can afford to give away free places!), and is an enterprise that rewards—and therefore fosters—excellence.

But mostly because you'll be able to advertise a scholarship in places that might never have allowed you to advertise your *studio*. The same shop that refused you permission to display a poster in the window about your studio (simply because it was perceived as merely an advertisement) may well soften when your pitch instead is that you have a poster advertising a *scholarship* to a deserving music student (which could be seen as more altruistic). Similarly, schools are much more likely to post such notices, music stores are more likely to put such notices front and center, and your local radio station may just be happy to chat to you about the scheme.

Such notices are also likely to be viewed more sympathetically by the readers. In a conventional advertisement, you create a document which raves about how great your studio is – and then hope that the reader is interested enough to take it all in. By contrast, if the document is the announcement of a scholarship, parents who might have an eligible child will see an *opportunity* straight away, and then are then going to be very interested to know more about what this opportunity would mean. In other words, they are going to *want* to read more about your studio. So you put the same rave down the bottom of the page, but this time, you know it will be read.

For those who miss out...

Independently of whether such students then apply for the scholarship, and then whether they actually get the scholarship, the message about your studio as a thriving place of excellence will have been absorbed. And then in the future, if these parents are looking for a change for whatever reason, your name will be in the running.

In fact, applying for a scholarship and not getting it can actually create quite a mystique surrounding your studio – *that to be there at all must be a privilege*. And so if they can't get there through the scholarship itself, then they may well consider enrolling through conventional means. It not only helps ensure fresh enquiries, but that the students themselves are prepared to work very hard once they come aboard.

MASTERCLASS: Lots of Mousetraps

No matter how excited you become by a particular promotion idea, it's important not to pin your hopes on any single technique. In short, it's easier to catch lots of mice if you set lots of mousetraps.

Even if each of your promotion ideas only has a one in ten chance of producing a phone call each day, by the time you have seven ideas out there working for you, this would mean that you have a better then even chance of your phone ringing on any given day.

In this way, every new promotion device you add *takes pressure off the others.* The logic is that instead of having just one tactic, and hoping it's a huge hit, you can have a dozen tactics that are all only mildly successful, and still enjoy the same outcome as a single huge-hit idea anyway.

> **If the only thing you have is a Yellow Pages ad, then you had better hope it's a sparkling piece of copywriting— because there are no reserve chutes if it fails.**

The power of diversity

Having lots of different *types* of mousetrap also spreads the risk—it allows you to have a promotion campaign item that is *not* so effective without your enquiries plummeting. If the only thing you have is a Yellow Pages ad, then you had better hope that it's a sparkling piece of copywriting, because there are no reserve parachutes if it fails to capture the imagination of would-be students.

The reality is that no matter how well you design your campaign, there is a chance that any given element within the campaign might not fire. The reason jumbo jets have so many engines is not because the plane needs them to fly—it's in case some of them fail. Built in redundancy like this is not redundant at all. It's there to protect you, and to give you permission to fail once in a while, without that failure having a catastrophic impact on your studio.

Combining your elements into a team

Every promotion campaign you have also needs to be *complemented* by the others. Their efforts have to be synchronized to produce a powerful bigger picture. As we'll see, the message you include in a Studio Website advertisement is very different from one you might post at your local shops, which is different again from the message you would give after presenting a concert at a nearby high school.

You need to regard each promotion idea as a team member, and to realize that each has a different role to play. Some campaign elements are just there to gently raise your profile, others are there to provide detailed background information for students who have already shortlisted your studio, while others are more aggressively marketing to new students.

But it's not just the *function* of the promotion elements that varies. They also will end up targeting different audiences. So within that body of potential students, some ads are targeted to first time students, others to potential transfer students, some are aimed at parents, while still others are actually aimed at other *teachers*.

With every element you select, you have to be able to answer the question "What's this *for?*"—and ensure that the answer is balanced with and supported by the roles of your other chosen elements, and consistent with your own goals for your studio. It's no good wishing that your studio would attract more adult beginners if none of your campaign elements are specifically targeting adults or beginners.

Think twice before discarding

Each time you decide *not* to use an idea, you have to be certain that it was a team member you didn't actually need. The real risk in promotion is not in the costs of the inclusion of a team member. It's in the danger of leaving members *out*, and taking the field minus your goalkeeper, one fullback, and two of your strikers.

Or worse still, taking the field with only *one* player – the same tired old player that brought in a trickle of enquiries last year, and the year before.

Sports analogies aside, if you stick to an existing non-effective formula, your results won't change either. Your waiting list is not going to grow by itself, and to bring about real change in your studio numbers, there has to be a real change in your approach to promotion.

Set another trap while you wait

Your new poster at the local school might take a few weeks to generate the enquiries you are hoping for, and even if your intention is to have plenty of other campaign elements, it can be tempting to stop all other promotion while you wait to see what impact your first idea has had.

Don't be lulled into inactivity as campaigns are launched. In the school scenario above, you should already be planning your new campaign *while the ink is still drying on the poster*. That way, if it becomes clear that the campaign is not working as effectively as you might have hoped, you have other options that are already hard at work for you.

Give free lessons during the holidays

You'd have to be mad. Giving away free lessons during the holidays? *Your* holidays!!

Obviously, your existing students cannot take advantage of this offer. But the idea is that anybody else can sign up for six free lessons over an intensive two week period. The maximum number of students you agree to take is up to you.

The aim of the six lessons is so parents who have been thinking about music lessons can put their toes in the water, without having any commitment concerns. By the end of the sessions, their kids will be able to play some tunes, read a little music, and hopefully be excited enough about the whole thing that it should be hard for everything to suddenly just stop there.

You would not be pushing for them to continue. In fact you would only refer to the whole thing as a terminating course. But if they want to make this positive experience a regular part of their lives, they will know where to find you.

And because their child already *knows* you, you will have the inside running if they decide to pursue lessons officially.

> **By the end of the sessions, the kids will be able to play some tunes, read a little music...**
>
> **...and hopefully be excited enough by the whole thing that it should be hard for everything to suddenly just stop there.**

It's not as if every child will continue. But if giving a dozen students lessons for free means that you end up with three new regular students, the whole thing will have been time very well spent.

And for those students who decide *not* to come aboard permanently, they may have siblings or friends who are looking for lessons in a year's time –again, your name will probably be the first that they think of.

Getting the word out

For this idea to be effective, parents need to know about it — which means you'll need to do some advertising. While this may feel like it's adding insult to injury (now you're suddenly *paying* money for people to have free lessons!), the advertisements themselves have a twin function. Not only will they help ensure that all places are filled for your free course, but they actually add to the profile of your studio in their own right.

Given that it's free, it might also be the sort of thing that a local school might be prepared to put in a newsletter. (Yet another reason to be fostering a good relationship with your local schools — see P 106)

Consider a multi-instrument sampler

One of the problems for parents is knowing which instrument is going to be right for their child, which creates a great opportunity for your free lessons holiday initiative to come to the rescue. If you *combine forces* with teachers of other instruments, you could offer participants a taste of half a dozen different instruments — a couple of lessons on each, so that they can experience the range of instruments for themselves.

> **If you combine forces with other instrumental teachers, you could offer participants a taste of half a dozen different instruments.**

At the end of that time, they should come away with a better idea of what's involved, together with a feeling for any of the instruments that just seemed to "click" straight away. This "sampler" approach would be a unique opportunity for parents considering music lessons, and again will give you the inside running for those students who ended up preferring the instrument you teach. (In fact, it's better than "inside running" — having enjoyed their time with you, the parents are highly unlikely to go anywhere else!)

Have brochures ready

Parents will generally be curious to find out more, and one of the points you will need to make is that while six lessons can feel exciting, it's only a pale shadow of what regular lessons can offer. To help them understand this, make sure you have brochures available — just the very fact that your studio actually *has* a brochure will create a good impression.

You should also refer them to your studio website. (You can create one for free at www.practicespot.com), together with providing them with information about what to do if they want the lessons to continue.

Put on a concert/information session

At the end of the six lessons, have a mini "graduation" concert. But this is not like your regular studio recitals. These are private concerts — for their own parent's ears only. You can then enthuse with the parents about how much their kids have already achieved, and then applaud with the parents after their child plays their very first piece. For the parents, it won't just be a sample lesson. It will be a Kodak Moment, and the fact that the piece might simply have consisted of a few middle Cs in a row won't worry them.

> **For many parents, it won't just be a sample lesson.**
>
> **It will be a Kodak Moment.**

You should also leave the parents with an understanding of what their kid already does *well*. Find something positive about the child's first few lessons, and give plenty of praise. It might be that they showed great concentration skills, or that they already produce a surprisingly good tone on the instrument, or that they got through more work than most people get through, or that their posture is unusually good. You're not just making up empty praise here — the feature you are highlighting is something that the child is genuinely good at. Even if they elect not to continue, you want the child leaving the studio walking a little taller than when they entered.

Faced with half a dozen lessons that their child really enjoyed, confirmation that their child has identifiable strengths for at least some aspect of the lessons, and evidence of progress in the form of the private mini concert, it will be a rare parent that wouldn't feel just a little sad if it all just ended there.

Leave them with a gift

To help keep music lessons part of the family's thinking for years to come, leave the student with a gift at the end of their sessions—a thank you for their participation.

> It all goes to building a compelling question in the parents' minds:
>
> If all of this is possible after only a few lessons, what would a few *years* of lessons produce?

It might be a specially printed T-Shirt, or a hat with a "My Very First Music Steps!" logo. It might be a signed copy of that very first piece that they played, or if you have the facilities, a recording.

If you have a studio website, take the time to write a note about each of the participants, making a fuss about the specific strengths that you had already identified to parents. Everyone loves seeing their name in print, and it will serve to reinforce the message that the child did a great job.

It all goes to building a compelling question in the parents' minds:

If all of this is possible after only a few lessons, what would a few years of lessons produce? Most of them will be consumed with curiosity to find out—and when they are ready to resume the adventure for real, it's you they'll call.

Teacher exchange program

It's a simple idea, it's free, and it can produce students when you least expect it. The idea is to contact other instrumental teachers — but *teachers specializing in instruments other than that which you teach* (otherwise it will look like a poaching attempt!) — and let them know that you want to swap studios for a couple of days. You would hear their students, they would hear yours.

An ideal time for this is in the lead up to a big recital or competition, where the second opinion might reinforce some messages the student needs to hear.

You might not know much about flute playing if you are a trombone teacher, but you know when someone's phrasing is good, or their intonation is poor. There's plenty you can talk about, short of actual technique — we're all musicians, after all.

> **It's all about profile. There are probably dozens of other instrumental teachers in town who would be happy to recommend you...**
>
> **... if only they knew you existed, and how much fun you are to work with.**

So how does it help?

Quite apart from helping out the other teacher, and having a positive impact on their students, a teacher exchange can make a big difference to your studio too.

Here's why.

Violin teachers get asked sometimes if they know any good singing teachers. Like pediatricians get asked if they know any good orthopedic surgeons. When questions come up about lessons for *your* instrument, your name should now spring to the mind of those teachers you have worked with.

More than that, if you are a clarinet teacher, that cellist you helped might have a little sister who wants to learn clarinet one day. Or a best friend.

It's all about profile. There are probably dozens of other instrumental teachers in town who would be happy to recommend you — if only they knew you existed, and how much fun you are to work with.

Extra options for piano teachers

Piano teachers are uniquely placed for this. As well as *hearing* other instrumentalists, they can volunteer to *accompany* students. Again, if the experience is positive for the accompanee, it is a short step for their teacher and their family to assume that piano lessons with you could be fun too.

Set up a musical "fitness circuit"

Instead of just limiting this exchange program to one teacher, you might find a group of four colleagues, and then have students rotate through the five of you over a five week period. You won't have to do any more teaching than you normally would, but you'll will end up with the chance to meet dozens of new students and their families.

The student may well be a violinist, but at the end of the four weeks, they will have test driven their upcoming program with a piano teacher, a french horn teacher, a jazz bass player and a singer — helping them think about their piece and performance in a fresh new way.

Like so many of the promotion strategies outlined in this book, this is an "everybody wins" idea. Students come out of it knowing their piece at a whole new level, and confident that it has survived a unique challenge.

You come out of it with dozens of families who now know your name, and that you're a great teacher. Not a bad outcome.

Target a niche

You're a flute teacher with good qualifications and years of experience? So are most of your competitors. Parents *might* choose you, but it's going to be lottery. Which means that a lot of potential students will be going to other teachers, *simply because all the studios seemed to be offering the same thing.*

It's time to stand out from the pack.

If there is a side of your teaching that you particularly enjoy, why not make it a studio *specialty*? There may be plenty of flute teachers around, but if you are the only one who mentions "special training in working with preschool kids!", then you'll probably be interviewed first by parents who want to get their kids off to an early start.

> **It's time to stand out from the pack.**
>
> **If there is a side of your teaching that you particularly enjoy, why not make it a studio *specialty*?**

Alternatively, you might make a point of mentioning that you are very experienced with nervous adult beginners, or theory students, or pre-college students wanting to secure entry to the conservatorium of their choice.

You might offer a "competition-free environment", or have a special focus on composing. You might be the only studio in town that teaches at night, or that runs special courses in teaching parents how to help their kids.

The downside can be that your studio might be perceived as *only* catering to your specialty—you will have to word things carefully.

But the upside is that not only will you have a huge advantage over other studios in attracting particular types of students, but that you will be stocking your studio with the students you enjoy working with most in any case! So if you bill your studio as being "friendly and gentle with students", then parents who value that approach will come to you. Not only that, but the parents who expect old-school taskmasters instead will probably call someone else after seeing your ad—which is a good thing, and heads off inevitable clashes before they begin. (If you genuinely value friendly and gentle lessons, then the parent wishing for a taskmaster was going to remove their child from your studio sooner or later anyway)

So in this way, targeting niches is not just an effective method of being noticed. It actually will filter enquiries so that most enquiries are about the thing you are *best* at. It makes the initial phone call easier, the interview easier, and then lessons easier.

Advertise your niche to other teachers

Every teacher will have particular types of students that they either don't enjoy working with, or recognize that they don't have the expertise to work with. When that happens, they may well be interested in passing such a student along to another teacher who could help.

Once you are clear on what your specialty is, make sure that all other teachers in your area know about the focus of your studio. Better still, run workshops for other teachers on that topic, helping stamp you as an expert in the subject.

The end result? When these teachers need to pass on a student to an expert in that area, you've ensured that you'll get the call.

So if your specialty is helping students who are having reading problems, the next time another teacher is at their wit's end over a student that can not and will not read, you might get the job instead. It provides an "out" for other teachers without them having to dump problem students—in fact, far from dumping, they are meeting their needs exactly by referring them to a specialist.

Create a network of niche referrals

Your niche should ensure that you are the only teacher in town who is a specialist in your particular area, but you won't be the only teacher in town with a niche of some sort. Yours might be working with very young beginners. Another studio's might be with adult students who are returning to lessons after a couple of decades' break. Another still might have an active interest in developing advanced aural skills.

Despite your best efforts at making your various niches clear in your ads, you'll still get calls from parents who are looking for something outside your area of expertise. To deal with such enquiries, the idea would be to establish a *network* of niche teachers based on reciprocating referrals.

So if you receive a call about an adult student who is resuming lessons after fifteen years off, instead of explaining that your studio really specializes in young kids and telling them to try someone else, you can give them the *name* of someone else. And not just anyone else—you can give them the name of the best expert available in their area.

> **In this way, everyone in the network is actively trawling for music students for you.**
>
> **Whenever their phone rings, there is a chance that *you* might actually end up with the student.**

Likewise, when other teachers in the network receive calls from parents with a four year old who wants music lessons, they'll pass on your name. In this way, everyone in the network is actively trawling for music students for you, and whenever their phone rings, there is a chance that *you* might actually end up with the student. This is useful if the network consists of a few teachers, but becomes a very exciting strategy if there are a dozen or more teachers involved.

Become involved with local schools

The days of every school having a music specialist are long gone, which creates an enormous opportunity for private music teachers with the willingness to volunteer. The decision to help out at a local school will make a big difference to the school concerned, and will be noticed by hundreds—maybe even thousands—of families.

How can you help? You can give a free concert to the Grade 5 students. Or be a special guest to hear the year 6 presentation on Great Composers. You can show the year 3 class how your trombone works, or run a Friday afternoon workshop for any kids who want to work on their note reading.

> **The decision to help out at a local school will make a big difference to the school concerned...**
>
> **...and will be noticed by hundreds—maybe even thousands—of families.**

You can assist by conducting the choir, or helping with rehearsals for the school musical presentation. You can run a little performance workshop on the first Tuesday in each month for anyone in the school who learns an instrument. Or a free music appreciation and listening club in the afternoons.

How much you do is up to you, but the greater your connection with the school, the higher your profile.

In the process, you will get to know hundreds of kids, and they will get to meet you too. If you do a great job, not only will they think of your name first if they are seeking lessons in the instrument you teach—they'll be much more likely to actually choose the instrument you teach in the first place.

Getting started

The first thing you should do is to send a letter to the Principal, outlining:

- Your **existing connection** to the school, by naming the students from the school that you teach.

- Introduce yourself as a resource, and that you are happy for the school to make use of you to help develop music at the school

- Who you are, background and qualifications

- Also make it clear that there will be **no charge** for the help

- **Ask for a meeting** at some stage to discuss what might be possible, together with any particular needs the school might have

> **Go into the meeting with one clear focus:**
>
> *How can I help?*

- Include half a dozen possibilities. Make it clear that it might not be possible to do all these things at once, but that they are certainly representative of how you can help

- Provide contact details and references should they need any further information

Follow up your letter a week later with a phone call to the Principal's office—make it clear that the meeting would only be exploratory in nature, and that you will not be assuming interest from the school just because they agree to speak with you. In other words, give them permission to find out more without feeling like they are committing themselves to anything.

Then go into the meeting with one clear focus:

"How can I help?"

Listen carefully to what they have to say, even if it was help of a nature that you had not anticipated. If they need someone to help catalogue the library's collection of books about composers, then so be it—it's a foot in the door, and you can expand from there.

107

Why go to all this trouble to help schools for free? Because the vast majority of your students — current and future — attend schools within a short drive of where you live.

If your profile at such schools is high enough, you may not *need* any other advertising. All it will take is the occasional note in the school newsletter indicating that your studio has space and will be interviewing soon for intake for next semester.

Cast a wide net

Unless your association with just one local school is already filling all your available time, you should consider extending similar offers to other institutions. Three schools is not necessarily three times the work — if your involvement is based around presenting concerts and workshops, you can re-use your material from one school to the next.

How your efforts can help you

Your focus should be very much on how you can help the school, but given time and the development of a relationship of trust, there are many ways in which the school can help promote your studio:

• The school is much more likely to allow you to **post notices** about upcoming student concerts, of even advertisements for places in the studio

• The school might agree to print an **acknowledgement** of your studio in programs for their productions — particularly if it was the production itself that you assisted with.

•The school might agree to have you present information sessions about your studio or student concerts in **their hall**, and waive any fees that might normally be associated with hall hire.

• They may even allow you to **teach at the school itself,** allowing you to regularly pitch to the students about how great music lessons can be. You win because you end up with a steady supply of students. They win because they can boast that their school offers music lessons to interested students.

• In the course of running your activities for the school, you will **meet hundreds of students** that you might never have otherwise, and in some cases, their families too. There is no better way to help people understand how rewarding and positive your lessons can be than to actually let them experience working with you for themselves.

• The school will be more receptive to the idea of having your students play for them — either at assembly, or perhaps at the annual fete.

> **Why go to all the trouble of helping schools for free?**
>
> **Because the vast majority of your students—current and future—live within a short drive of where you live.**

• Whenever parents have a query about the possibility of music lessons, all the staff at the school will not only know who you are, but will be able to actively and warmly recommend you.

• Unlike so many other promotion ideas, providing assistance to local schools won't cost you a cent. It's a mutual back scratching exercise that provides the school with help and expertise that they might not have had access to otherwise, and provides profile and opportunity for you that you could never get with a mere advertisement.

MASTERCLASS: Call on your strengths

Before you start selecting the various elements for your campaign, you need to make sure they are working *with* your own particular strengths and weaknesses—not against them.

A music teacher with a public speaking phobia but good desktop publishing skills should probably steer clear of the "Present your own Seminar" strategy, but may well be able to achieve stellar results with a color brochure and letterbox drop. Similarly, a teacher with good networking skills would be ideal to launch a new music competition, while someone who was more introverted but with a flair for writing might want to try a piece for the local paper (all these ideas—and many—others are explained later in the book!).

> **You have to use the cards you have been dealt as effectively as possible.**
>
> **But you can't do that until you've had a good look at what those cards *are*.**

Some of the strengths and weaknesses you need to consider will actually be environmental. So for example, organizing free concerts at your local school is less effective if the school is already saturated with music and music teachers, but you might find that the local Pre-Schools might not be so well equipped musically, and might jump at the opportunity. Likewise, if you live in a major metropolitan center, a huge Yellow Pages display ad might cost you more than a new car, but a short interview on radio would be free and worth its weight in gold. The reverse would be true if you live in a small country town that has two digit phone numbers.

Every time there is a change in your own skill base or environment, you need to reassess your promotion strategies. In other words, once you stumble on a successful promotion idea, you can't simply assume that it will *always* be appropriate.

Being smart about your choices

This book provides a huge range of ideas because there is a huge range of teachers. Your own profile and preferences will be unique, so it was never going to be possible to create a "one-size-fits-all" advertising campaign for everyone who reads this book. Successful promotion will be about *choosing* strategies that call on your strengths, and using the cards you have been dealt as effectively as possible. You can't do that until you've had a good look at what those cards are.

Rate the ideas for compatibility

Not compatibility with each other. Compatibility with *you*.

For every idea you read in the second half of this book, make a note of what **personal** **qualities** would be required for you to pull the idea off successfully. Do they require good telephone manner? Or the willingness to cold-call potential strategic partners? Or strong layout and design skills? Or the touch of a wordsmith? Or perseverance? Or the willingness to work with the media? Or knowledge of computers? Or strong organizational skills? Or confidence in front of a crowd?

You should also list the required **resources**. Does the idea require a good printer, or the co-operation of your students, or a large hall? Does it require plenty of cash up front, or a lot of free time?

Armed then with a list of what's required for each idea, you can match that against your own personal qualities and resources. This should then convert dozens of possible promotion strategies into a short list of those that you are best suited to delivering successfully.

And those ideas that rate poorly on this compatibility index? Make a note of what exactly you are missing to make such an idea a reality, and consider a little upgrading—either of your own skills, or your available resources. There's no reason that a snapshot of your current skills and resources has to be representative of what will be available to you in two years' time.

Strategic partnerships with music stores

It's this simple. Your local music stores would love your studio to be *overflowing* with students. Not because they're nice people, but because every new student you get is going to need metronomes and music books, manuscript paper and theory drills. They're going to need to buy new instruments, and upgrade the ones they've already got. And that's not taking into account the world of music software, midi instruments, sound cards or recording equipment. In short, if you do well, some music stores nearby are going to do *very* well. (Probably much better than you!)

Every time they create a new student for you, they create a new customer for themselves.

Which is a powerful incentive for them to be creating new students for you in the first place.

The only problem is, they know that your students are free to shop from a variety of different stores. What you can offer them is an exclusive recommendation for their music store—so that if you were a clarinet teacher, and your 4 pm Wednesday student needs to buy new reeds and is asking where to get them, you have an answer ready for her. You probably even have a brochure with a map.

In return, when someone buying sheet music asks the counter staff if they can recommend any good clarinet teachers, your name will come up.

In this way, every time they create a new student for you, they create a new customer for themselves. Which is a powerful incentive for them to be creating new students for you in the first place.

Negotiating outside the square

Such partnerships can go beyond simple mutual recommendations. Once your studio fills up, you may even be able to negotiate a special discount for your students — the idea being that if they mention your studio's name when purchasing, the store will give them 5% off the purchase price. In return, you might agree to do an in-store promotion of their new line of clarinets, answering questions from customers who want to hear from a true expert.

The extent to which the relationship develops is up to you and the store manager. They may agree to lend you brand new instruments in return for your testimonial. They may provide you with a certain amount of free sheet music each year in return for you providing in-store workshops. As the relationship develops, so will the enthusiasm with which they will promote your studio.

After all, if you are advertised as being the "expert teacher" who is coming in for a free workshop the first Sunday of each month, then they are going to want to ensure that your name has pulling power. Which means they are going to have to promote the living daylights out of your name, and your studio.

Everybody wins.

Swap brochures

Given the symbiotic relationship between the two businesses, it makes sense for you both to be armed with plenty of information about each other. When your students ask where to buy a new instrument, you can tell them the name of the store, confirm that you have bought new instruments there for years, enthuse about how the staff know what they're talking about, and then provide a brochure that might answer any further questions they might have about models, finance plans etc.

Similarly, the music store would have your brochure available for any enquiries about music lessons. (It's amazing how often people buy the instrument first, and then look for teachers afterwards!).

Exchange advertising space

The next time you have a student recital, you can offer to include a small advertisement for the music store on the program itself. In return, the store might agree to display a poster advertising your studio near their front counter, or leave a bunch of brochures for your studio near the sheet music section for the instrument you teach.

You can't expect exclusivity — meaning that your brochures may well be side by side with those of other teachers. But you'll still have an advantage over those many studios that are not represented at all.

Create a joint event

This is an idea that is probably more open to you once you have established a profile in town, but is a great way of helping maintain that profile. The idea would be to hold a presentation at the store itself — you would provide the expertise, and would be the drawcard for parents or teachers to turn up in the first place. (As one of the bigger studios in town, there will be plenty of people who will be curious to hear what you have to say)

The store would provide the venue, and might also want to use part of the session to promote a new gadget or line of sheet music. Advertising would also be the responsibility of the store, perhaps in partnership with the manufacturer of any products that the session might be promoting.

So how does it help? In order to use your name as a drawcard for the event, they will need to feature it prominently in the advertisement, together with a line or two about why you're a drawcard in the first place — which means saying nice things about you.

The end result? They end up with a free seminar that brings people into their store, and helps label them in the community as supporting music in the town. You end up with high-profile free advertising, together with the accompanying assumption that if you've been invited to do this, then you must be an expert indeed.

Make use of your car

Businesses pay plenty of money each year to have their message displayed on the side of buses or the backs of taxis. The logic is that motorists stuck in traffic end up reading the messages whether they want to or not — when we're going nowhere, our eyes tend to wander, and we read pretty much anything that's available. (It's the same reason that home-decorating magazines from 1983 suddenly seem fascinating when you're in a doctor's waiting room)

Instead of paying to have such ads on other people's vehicles, pay a signwriter to put one on yours.

I'm serious.

Many teachers are resistant to this idea, because it feels like a "trade" tactic — for plumbers and carpenters, not artists like music teachers. But if you want to fill your studio, you can't afford to be precious like that. The advertisement will only be tacky if the message is — there's nothing wrong with the medium. Make the message fun, unusual, and memorable, and the ad will do its job.

> **Every time you go shopping, when you sit in traffic jams, while you wait in line at a drive-through...**
>
> **...your car is helping the studio name achieve a ring of familiarity.**

And then, every time you go shopping, when you sit in traffic jams, while you wait in line at a drive-through, your car is helping the studio name achieve a ring of familiarity. It's not as though people will suddenly grab their phone and book their whole family in for music lessons because they happened to be behind your station wagon at Burger King. But when the time does come for music lessons, and they see your ad in the Yellow Pages, your name will sound somehow…familiar…but they probably won't be able to quite put a finger on it.

When that happens, and they call you, go out and pat your car gently on the hood. It's done good work for you.

115

Get some bumper stickers printed

You certainly shouldn't try to mandate it, but the big advantage with having a pile of promotional bumper stickers available is that some of your students might be happy to put them on their *own* cars.

Most copy shops should be able to create the bumper stickers for you fairly inexpensively, and you can leave the pile prominently in your studio. Those students that are interested will take one, helping your car-borne advertising to be in several places at once.

Alternatively, you might offer a fee discount for any parent who agrees to display your bumper sticker. Don't ask the parents directly—instead simply include it as an offer in your newsletter. That way you're not setting up an awkward situation where they might have to say "no" to you—if they are not interested, all they have to do is do nothing, allowing everyone to save face.

It's also worth considering holding a studio Bumper Sticker design competition amongst your students—offer prizes for the five best entries, and a grand prize for the winning submission. Even if nobody else displays the bumper sticker, the winner of the competition is highly likely to want to display their own handiwork—and you've just doubled the number of cars in town that display ads for your studio.

Reciprocal promotion with other child-based businesses

Advertising of any sort is a lot more effective if it is targeted. You may well have delivered 2,000 leaflets about music lessons, but if your studio specializes in working with kids, and 1,500 of your leaflets went to households with no children, then you might as well have sent out 1,500 blank sheets of paper.

The easiest way to target your message to people who might be interested in it is to go where those people are likely to be. Because most music students tend to be children, you need to find *parents* – and they're not hard to locate.

> **Because most music students tend to be children, you need to find *parents*—and they're not hard to locate.**

They're at day care centers. They're at junior softball games. They're at toyshops. They're at indoor adventure playgrounds, and kid's clothes shops, and junior chess tournaments, and math tutors, and ice skating rinks.

You need to establish reciprocal promotion arrangements with businesses like these. Ask to find out more about their business, and find out how you can help promote them to your students. Tell them you are happy to have their business card or brochure available in your waiting area, and ask them if they can display yours.

You might even agree to give two free lessons to any one of their clients who contacts you for an interview, instead of the usual one.

Likely candidates

The best place to start is with activities that one or more of your students is already involved with. Approach a local horseriding club, and when you introduce yourself, mention the names of your students who are actually learning to ride here, and that they talk non-stop about it during their music lessons. (If they're learning to ride a horse, they probably *do* talk non-stop about it at lessons!) Tell them that you're here to find out more, and ask if they have any brochures that you can leave for students who ask you about horseriding. And let them know that you are very interested to explore ways in which your studio and their school can help promote each other.

Not everyone will say yes. But as with all your promotion strategies, the one guarantee that is in place is that if you don't ask, *nothing* will happen. You can't afford to be the person who is too shy to ask anyone to dance—even if only *one* business says "Sure! Great idea—leave me with some posters", and even if that poster only brings in one student, your approach has ended up being worth hundreds of dollars each year.

Keep local media informed about student successes

When the local media features a story about a kid who came second in a state archery competition, it's not because the sports editor was out chasing the story. It's because the kid's archery club contacted *them*. The vast majority of "success story" type news comes about because the media was informed about it by a person or organization associated with the successful person.

Next time you have a student who performs well in a concerto competition, or is a finalist in a composition competition, don't just publish the fact in your studio newsletter. Put together a press release, and send it to local media. They might run it, they might not. But if you don't send it in the first place, you are *guaranteeing* that they won't run it.

You can make it easier for them by providing all the details in the release itself, together with any scanned photographs on disk. Sometimes editors with a tight deadline looming won't go for the best story — they go for a story that will be easy to write. You never know, your story might just be what they need to fill that awkward space on page twelve.

> **Next time you have a student who performs well in a concerto competition, or is a finalist in a composition festival...**
>
> **...don't just publish the fact in your studio newsletter.**

If a story does run, it's tremendously exciting for all concerned. Not only does it provide a well-deserved public pat on the back for the student, it also provides a tremendous boost to your studio's profile. The student will be forever grateful that you took the time to organize the publicity, and will have yet another reason for wanting to stay in your studio. And you can put the icing on the cake by cutting out the clipping to add to your Wall of Fame in your studio, so that prospective students can see it during the interview, and so that existing students can be inspired during their lesson.

Everybody wins, and it costs you nothing but the courage to submit the news.

Keep schools informed too

Much like the media, schools can only highlight the successes of their students *if they know about those successes.* Your student may well have just won second place in a flute competition, but you can't simply assume that they will tell the school about it.

It's up to you to make that phone call or visit. Bring some details of the triumph, so that it will be easy for the principal to gush at assembly.

Most principals are delighted to hear about the achievements of students, and your student certainly won't mind basking in the extra glory. Taking the time to notify the school like this helps boost the profile of the student at school (which helps the student), provides the school with someone they can hold up as Role Model of the Week (which helps the school), and prompts the question as to who this child's music teacher is (which helps you).

It's another everybody-wins scenario, and also helps make the student a celebrity for a day among their peers. Everyone likes to have their name mentioned at assembly, and this promotion technique will not only raise your profile, but will probably have your students practicing harder afterwards too.

What sorts of achievements are newsworthy?

You don't need to wait until a student wins a major international competition, or has a new recital hall at Julliard named after them. Any time they have a success that has a tangible reward — a ribbon, a trophy, a place, a certificate — it's something the school should not only know about, but actually *see.* Not only is your studio benefiting from the extra exposure, but new support networks and interest will spring up for that student at school. When a teacher on playground duty chats with them, instead of just making small talk about what a nice day it is, they'll probably ask the student how their music lessons are going.

All of which makes it much, much harder for them to quit — thus having a subtle but positive impact on your retention rates. In other words, the few minutes you took to keep the school up to date on a high achieving student could have an impact for years to come.

If all else fails, post it yourself

Independently of whether or not the local paper decides to run your stories about student successes, you should consider taking out an annual ad that highlights student achievements from the year that was. These achievements don't have to be competition victories. You might mention the hardest practicers, the most improved intermediate students, or the best new student. In other words, you'll be *creating* categories so that you can mention as many of your students as possible (in fact, you should really be trying to mention *all* of them!)

It's similar to the awards that you might have handed out anyway after an end-of-year

> **You don't need to wait until a student wins a major international competition, or has a new recital hall at Julliard named after them.**

recital, but the acknowledgements this time are very public. Which means they can serve two functions.

Not only will those students be bursting with pride (everyone loves seeing their name in the paper!), *but the ad will also be noticed by parents of potential students*. This advertisement won't need to say anything about your studio except the studio name at the top — the very existence of such a public acknowledgement of your students' efforts will tell parents more good things about your studio than your most eloquent copywriting could.

And as an added bonus, knowing that the ad exists is a powerful incentive for students who are already in your own studio. They'll want their name in lights again this year, and will practice just a little harder to ensure it happens.

Create a resource—and sell it through a local music store

Music teachers tend to be a fairly creative bunch, and it's not unusual for us to build our own resources for use in lessons.

Whether it's practice games, rhythm reading sheets, scales charts, specially designed stickers or posters, name-that-composer board games, or our own unique flash cards, don't just use them with the students you already have. It's time to use these creations to excite students you've never even met.

> **It's time to use your creations to excite students you've never even met.**

How? The next time you come up with a useful resource, spend a little extra time on the presentation, *and then approach your local music store with it.* Seriously. Not as a money spinner—you would be supplying it for next to nothing—but as a promotional tool. The store can sell it for whatever they like, but the item itself would clearly have the name of your studio on it.

Even if customers are not actively purchasing your creation, just having it available at the store says more about the creativity and enterprise of your studio than a simple advertisement ever could. You win because of the extra profile your studio gets. And the store wins because they can stock a unique item with a generous margin.

Possibilities for sale

What sorts of resources might interest your local store? *Anything that they don't already have in abundance.* The fact that you may have built a scales chart might excite you, but if they already have five different versions from their existing suppliers, they're not going to want to chat to you about a sixth.

On the other hand, if yours is the very first chart they have that is obviously aimed at absolute beginners, or the first that's designed for jazz students, then they have a selling point. If you expect the store to go to the trouble of including your masterpiece on their valuable shelf space, then you have to make it easy for them to recommend it, and to be clear about exactly who they would be recommending it to.

Allow them to refuse

As with all approaches to other businesses, you don't want to be pushy at all. Your resource is there for them if they are interested, and if they are not, they have to be able to say "no thank you" without any further argument from you. Apart from anything else, you're almost certainly going to want to approach them again one day about something else, and you don't want them hiding under the counter as you enter the store.

Seek publishers for your best efforts

If you really want to have your creations labelling you as an expert, talk to some publishers about having your resource printed and distributed through traditional channels. Not only would publication add extra credibility to your resource, but it would allow the resource to appear in stores that you could not approach personally.

It's one thing to be able to mention in your advertising that your theory book is available at your local music store. It's quite another when it's available nationwide, or *worldwide* through Amazon.com—a publisher can help make that happen. Again, be ready to collect plenty of rejection slips along the way, and remember that there are lots of publishers out there. (Even Harry Potter was rejected by several publishers...so don't think badly of your creation just because it wasn't right for the first publisher you approached).

Again it's about standing out from the pack. How many music teachers are represented in music stores in this way?

Advertise student concerts

Your student concerts may well be an in-house affair, with small audiences of grandmas, grandpas and invited friends, sitting alongside proud video-camera-carrying parents—but they don't *have* to be so insular.

A few weeks before the big day, it's time to get the word out that the concert is coming. Not just to remind your students, *but to bring the event to the attention of potential new students too.*

Put posters up in local shops, perhaps even place an ad in a local paper—if you want posters *everywhere*, then simply run a competition with your students. Tell them that there is a fabulous prize awaiting for the student who can display the most *prominent* poster advertising the concert, and another for the student who can get posters into the greatest number of shop windows. And another competition for designing a great poster in the first place.

> **None of these brochures or advertisements will say "Come and have lessons at this studio!".**
>
> **They don't need to, because a concert speaks for itself...and it says good things.**

Supercharging the atmosphere

If you want this concert to be an event that stays in the minds of potential students long after the last note dies away, it's time to stage manage the occasion. Encourage your students to bring a cheer squad of friends from school—tell them that you will be handing out special awards for "most applause for a student", and that they had better start stacking the audience. Their job is turn up with an army of supporters, and for those supporters to go absolutely nuts when the student actually walks on stage. Whistling, feet stamping, the works. This is no time for modest ripples of applause. It should be like the Beatles arriving at an airport for the first leg of a tour.

Not only will it have a tremendous impact on the size and enthusiasm levels of the audience, it can provide a tremendous confidence boost for the students on the receiving end of all this. They're not likely to forget a welcome to the stage like *that* in a hurry, and they'll be all smiles before their first note is played.

But most of all, the atmosphere of excitement and positive energy won't be lost on any potential students who are there either. The thought in their minds? That could be *me* up there.

Getting potential students to turn up

You concert has the potential to be a student-winning event, but posters alone won't fill the hall with curious prospective parents. Let your local newspaper and radio station know about the concert — the pitch being that for all those parents who are considering music lessons for their child, there will be a concert showcasing what's possible. Free admission, free afternoon tea, good music, and the chance to perhaps inspire your own kids into doing something similar. Make it clear that you'll be available afterwards to take questions from parents who are considering starting the music lessons adventure — no matter what instrument they are considering learning. Better still, if you have a particularly young student, mention them and their age. When listeners hear that a couple of the performers are

> **When listeners hear that a couple of the performers are only four, they'll look at their *five* year old and wonder what might be possible.**

only *four*, then they'll look at their five year old and wonder what might be possible.

This whole exercise is a good example of indirect promotion for your studio. None of the brochures, posters or other advertisements for the concert will say "Come and have lessons at this studio!". They don't need to, because the concert speaks for itself, and it says good things.

125

Organize a practice-a-thon

It's a simple enough idea. Your students will be raising money for a worthy cause, practicing hard in pursuit of that end, and building the profile of your studio while they do.

> **Your efforts won't just be advertising your studio.**
>
> **They'll be genuinely helping other people too.**

But it's not just about promotion. If you have twenty students who raise an average of $50 each, then that's a $1,000 (!) check your studio is going to be able to present to a charity/ hospital/school. Quite apart from the photo-op at the check handover, that $1000 is going to provide tangible assistance to the organization itself. So your efforts won't just be advertising your studio – they'll be genuinely helping other people too.

There are two ways you can run this.

The traditional fund-raiser

Students acquire sponsors who will agree to donate a set amount for every hour of practice the student completes during a defined two week period. You would need to make up a special sheet on which they can record sponsors' details, and also record their own practice times. Your students then go into a sponsor-gathering and practicing frenzy, and because we've all participated in "...athons" of one sort or another as kids, it will feel like familiar territory for them.

You can help add a little incentive by offering prizes to students who raise the most money, and then giving public acknowledgement of the leading fundraisers in your studio newsletter or website.

Fund-raising in the Spotlight

The second option is a little more complicated to set up, but can make for more of an "event". Instead of all that practicing happening in the student's homes, *it's going to take place somewhere public* — a shopping center or train station for example. And they're not just doing some practice. The idea is that students from your studio would play *continuously* for 48 hours. Scales, pieces, improvisations, whatever. They'd operate in shifts, but the plan is that between them, there would be no break in the music until the 48 hours is up. Members of the public can contribute to the cause simply by "purchasing" a sticker or badge. The funds collected in this way go straight to the cause.

And those stickers or badges? As well as saying "Practice-a-thon" and the name of the cause that's being supported, they also have (in smaller print) the name of your studio. As will the poster that is behind the students. As will the T-shirt your students wear while they are playing. As will the banner in the background of the photo as the check is handed over. The point is that if you make the event a success, it becomes a very powerful vehicle for promoting the name of your studio.

The advantage of an event-based Practice-a-thon like this is that it's more likely to be of interest to the media. Even if they don't agree to an interview, it's the sort of thing that could get a mention:

"For those of you who can never seem to get your kids to practice, you might want to turn up your radios for a second—this weekend 25 students from the Henderson School of Music will be playing for *48 hours straight* in support of cancer research. You can support this music marathon outside Starbucks on the 3rd level of Century Mall."

This is a much more powerful advertisement for the Henderson School of Music than an ad ever could have been — even though nothing has been said directly about school of music itself. The very existence of a Practice-a-thon speaks volumes about the initiative and creativity of the studio, with no further editorials required.

Letterbox Drop

A letter box drop is an effective, but somewhat blunt weapon in any studio promotion campaign, because despite the best demographic estimates, there is no way of accurately profiling any given household that will receive your advertisement.

It's great if the ad happens to go to a family that has been thinking about music lessons for some time. They might even call.

But it's not so useful if the same note goes to a biker named "Thor" in the apartment below whose only musical experience was to have contracted industrial deafness from a death metal concert in his teens. He's probably not going to be taking flute lessons any time soon.

> **Outside of major tertiary music programs, the vast majority of music studios specialize in working with students who live *nearby***

In other words, despite your best efforts on the brochure, a lot of people who read your ad will have no reason to be interested in it, and will dispose of it just the same way they dispose of every other catalogue and sales pitch that invades their mailbox.

This doesn't say bad things about you or your teaching. Nor does it necessarily imply anything negative about a Letterbox Drop as an advertising medium. It simply reflects the reality that the service you offer was only ever going to interest a minority of people anyway—even if you happen to be the most celebrated teacher of your instrument on the planet.

Being prepared for redundancies

The end result is that you have to be ready to put out a *lot* of brochures, and to accept that if even 5% of the recipients actually read it, then you're doing well. And of those, maybe only 5% again will be interested enough to *keep it*. Using those numbers—which in some suburbs will be generous—if you send 500 out, *499 would be trashed.* The vast majority of what you sent has just become landfill.

Guilt trips about wasted paper aside, there is one important way in which a letterbox drop is highly targeted though, and which alone is sufficient reason to seriously consider including such a strategy in any promotion campaign...

> **No matter how fast they throw the ad out, a subtle message about the standards of your studio will have been absorbed.**

...*all of the recipients will live nearby.* It sounds trivial, but it's not. Outside of major tertiary music programs, the vast majority of music studios specialize in working with students who in the same neighborhood. Not because the teacher prefers to work with local students, *but because a lot of parents don't want to have to travel too far for what would be a weekly commitment. (see p 70)*

A letterbox drop will ensure that everybody who is both

a) within walking distance of your studio, and

b) interested in music lessons

will have seen your message—even if it was just a cursory glance before they wrapped some vegetable peels with it.

As we'll see, a cursory glance is actually all you need.

The secondary impact

So what then of these 499 discarded fliers? Were your efforts wasted because your ad was thrown away 99.8% of the time?

Not at all. You don't need people to put your ad on their fridge for it to have done its job.

Every ad you circulate increases the chance that your studio's name will have a familiar ring about it when the time *does* come to pursue lessons. Your letterbox drop might not be enough. Your Yellow Pages ad might not be enough. Your interview on the radio might not be enough. But all three combined start to create a definite presence for would-be students, even if you cannot put a finger on which promotion technique was the clincher.

So while a letterbox drop is not going to suddenly have neighbors around you considering music lessons for the first time in their lives, it will help remind those who *are* considering music lessons of something very important:

"I'm here, I offer great music lessons– and *I'm just around the corner!*"

The radius for your drop

So how wide an area should a letterbox drop cover? It's easy to work out—anywhere that is more than 15 minutes walk away is going to start to stretch your "local" claim. For households outside that zone, you need to either consider alternative advertising techniques, or a toning down of the "nearby" references in your copy.

That having been said, unless you're living in a semi-rural area, there are normally a staggering number of households within a 15 minute walking radius. If only a tiny percentage of them signed up for lessons, you'd actually find yourself swamped.

Making it look professional

As for any other print based promotion ideas, your studio will be judged by the ad's *appearance*, no matter how proud you might be of the message inside. Don't be frustrated by this "judge a book by its cover" syndrome though—it's actually the reason that your ad will work for all 500 households. If your brochure is imaginative, polished and professional, *then the assumption will be that your studio is too.*

In short, if your ad looks great, no matter how fast households throw it out, a subtle and positive message about the standards of your studio will have been absorbed.

MASTERCLASS: Learn from other ads

Like everybody else, you will be bombarded each day by ads from dozens of different sources. Instead of simply resenting the invasion of your letterbox/email intray/television/cereal packet, use it as an opportunity to learn from the promotion ideas of others.

So the next time a mailout brochure catches your eye, rather then has you heading straight for the trash, ask yourself what it was about the ad that gave you pause. It might the layout, or the use of color, or the enigmatic text on the front fold, or the unusual logo. It could be the way it was folded, or addressed, or the type of paper it was printed on.

In this way, you don't just have to *admire* the clever promotion work of others. You can *copy* it. Many of the world's most successful advertising campaigns are simply reworkings of existing campaigns. It's the reason that advertising agencies are always keeping an eye on the ads that their competitors produce, as well as scouring less well known sources from other countries.

> **You don't just have to *admire* the clever promotion work of others.**
>
> **You can *copy* it.**

So when your Yellow Pages listing comes out, don't just admire your own handiwork. Get to know the copy, layout, content, style and tone of every other music teacher listing. Highlight those ads that you think are successful, analyze the elements that made them so effective, and then ask how you can use similar techniques to improve your own ad. Alternatively, you can also use such analysis to ensure that your ad is completely different from any other around, helping it stand out from the crowd—either way, the content of next year's ad can be shaped by your awareness of the efforts of your colleagues *this* year.

You don't just have to limit this sort of analysis to ads for music lessons. Open the Yellow Pages anywhere at random, and ask yourself what works and what doesn't. Steal the best ideas, rework them, and release them next year in your new improved ad.

Every time a new offer, bumper sticker, slogan or pitch captures your attention, take a moment to identify what makes it tick. Like every other human endeavour, successful advertising is made much easier if you are prepared to learn from the triumphs and disasters of others. And if your focus happens to be advertising, you won't run short of source material to research.

Start with replicas

Having reverse-engineered some effective advertisements, the next step is to actually build a *replica*, but with your content inserted. You shouldn't risk actually using it without making some further changes, but in the same way that painters sometimes learn by copying the works of the masters, you'll learn a lot about layout and copy simply by replicating existing masterpieces. You'll also discover a thing or two about any desktop publishing deficiencies you may have—sometimes ads that look simple and striking can be hard to construct. But once you've worked it out, it's then another technical trick you can add to your arsenal.

Keep a scrapbook

When you have ads to create and limited time to work with, you don't want to have to sit tapping a pencil against your head as you try to remember some of these great ideas you've seen in the past.

Instead of tossing away the work of others once you've analyzed it, add it to a Great Advertising Ideas scrapbook. The next time the creative juices are refusing to flow, spend a few minutes browsing the scrapbook—it's amazing how often ideas will leap out at you once it's all sitting in front of you.

Become active in your local MTA

It's simple really — if other teachers don't know who you are, they can't recommend you.

But there's a more compelling reason to be involved in your local MTA. When you are in constant touch with other teachers, you will be more aware of opportunities that could boost your profile, and the profile of music lessons generally. There are workshops to run, competitions to organise or adjudicate, concerts to introduce — if you take the time to find out about these things, and then get involved with them, your name will be familiar to all the families who attend.

> **When you are in constant touch with other teachers, you will be more aware of opportunities that could boost your profile - and the profile of music lessons generally.**

I am not saying that because you were known as the person who organised the Winter Workshop 2003 that all the participants will suddenly ditch their existing teachers and join your studio. But for their families, you are at least (to some extent) now a known quantity, in what otherwise can be a blind fishing expedition through a sea of music teacher advertisements. And if it leads to just *one* student that might otherwise not have even contacted you, the afternoon spent is well worth while.

Of course, the other side effect of participating in your local Music Teacher Association is that you will end up being a better teacher — you will meet a LOT of great ideas that you might not have heard of otherwise. While this might not help make new students stream through the door, it will make it much easier to keep the ones you already have.

Offer "free lessons" as a raffle prize

The next time a local school is organizing a raffle to help support the purchase of new computers, don't just sit on the sidelines. Offer free lessons at your studio as a prize.

It doesn't need to be a whole year – a dozen free lessons should be plenty, and would be ideal for parents who want a taste of music lessons for their child without having to commit to anything longer term.

> **The total cost to you is a few hours of your time - but there are plenty of benefits.**

The total cost to you is a few hours of your time, but there are plenty of benefits.

First of all, your studio name will be appearing on thousands of tickets, together with any advertising of the raffle itself. So if the raffle is mentioned on radio, the prizes are likely to be mentioned too, which is a free on-air plug for your studio.

Secondly, it creates a perception in your local community that you are actually active in and support that community. You don't *have* to donate six hours of your time to giving music lessons to a raffle winner, and the fact that you did will be noted.

And finally, there is a good chance that the student who has the twelve free lessons will then stay on and become a regular member of your studio. Which means that you end up new permanent addition to your teaching schedule for your troubles.

Alternatives

The prize you offer doesn't have to be free practical lessons. You might offer free theory tuition, or free tutoring for students who simply want to excel in their upcoming music finals at school. If your studio specializes in teaching composing or improvisation, you might agree to write a song as a prize – let the raffle winner supply the words, you put it together into music as an unforgettable Valentine's Day surprise.

Alternatively you might decide not to offer services of any sort, but instead provide a free subscription to all symphony concerts in town this year — sponsored by your studio. There are plenty of possibilities, and for inspiration, all you need to do is take note of prizes on offer in the various raffles you encounter.

Finding suitable raffles

Raffles don't just happen — they take plenty of organisation, and you have to be aware that contributors will have been decided long before the first tickets go on sale.

In other words, by the time you are aware of any given raffle, it's already too late to be involved.

That's no reason to be discouraged, it is a reminder that a raffle is the type of campaign that you plan now so that it can happen next year. You need to spend *this* year collecting information about existing raffles, and then sending them a proposal to be considered as a prize for the next year.

As ever, try to find causes and activities that complement the music lessons you offer. A local junior softball team that is raising money for an interstate trip is a good prospect. But a school band trying to finance a similar trip is even better.

Create a brochure that explains exactly what your proposed prize offers, together with some information about your studio. The same brochure should also include the One Sentence version of the prize, so that you are in control over how your contribution will be acknowledged in any advertising of the raffle itself. Make sure your contact details are prominent, together with an indication that you are happy to discuss (and perhaps tailor) the specifics of the prize with the organizing committee .

Plenty of raffles won't be interested, or would not be prepared to offer your studio the profile you are seeking in return. That's ok. There is no shortage of raffles to target — keep your eyes open, and chase the most promising prospects hard.

Give a free seminar for parents

Parents considering music lessons for their kids often have no musical background of any sort themselves. They have no idea of what to expect, nor of what expectations will be placed upon them. They'll be dimly aware that there will be books and metronomes to buy, but probably have never heard of a reed, bow-resin. or valve oil. They'll know that their child is supposed to "practice", and that as parents, their support of that practice is central to the success of the lessons—but they won't know what that support should consist of.

> **If you get the presentation right, it will be a more powerful advocate for your studio than any sales pitch could have been.**

They will probably have heard of Suzuki and Kindermusik and maybe perhaps even Kodaly. But they won't know what they mean. And they'll know that there is an entire orchestra of instruments to choose from, but won't know which one will be right for their child.

All of this provides a unique promotion opportunity for any music teacher with some initiative and a flair for public speaking. The aim would be to put together a *free information evening*, designed specifically for parents who are considering music lessons, but don't know where to start. In the process, you become a highly public expert on music tuition—in fact, for everybody in the room who is considering the instrument *you* teach, *you'll instantly become the teacher they know best*. Which means that when the time comes for these parents to start interviewing studios, you'll be at the top of their shortlist.

There are some cautions though. This session needs to be a genuine and free service for anyone who is considering music lessons, whatever the instrument, and whatever the reason. You need to be very careful not to turn the whole thing into an ad for your studio—in fact you probably shouldn't even *mention* your studio.

If you get the presentation right, it will be a more powerful advocate for your studio than any sales pitch could have been anyway. They'll see you in action, recognize that you know what you're talking about, and have an opportunity to actually meet you afterwards.

As a promotion exercise, you couldn't hope for more.

Preparing your presentation

Long before you fire up PowerPoint and start rehearsing your opening flourishes, you need to be very clear on what your audience will learn from all of this. Your starting point is to create a list of questions that parents might reasonably ask, and the more you can think of the better:

- How much practice should my child do?
- Which instrument is best for a very young child to learn?
- How much are music lessons likely to cost?
- What are the benefits or disadvantages of group lessons?
- What actually happens in a music lesson?
- How can I help my child practice at home?
- What will my child need apart from an instrument?
- How important it is it to have a quality instrument?
- What do you know about the "Mozart Effect"?
- Should my child be playing classical or contemporary music?
- How can we set up a good practice room for my child?
- How young is too young to start?
- Should I sit in on lessons?
- What should I look for in a teacher?
- What questions should I ask in an interview?
- How do I know my child is actually ready for music lessons?
- Which instrument should my child play?
- How difficult is instrument X,Y or Z?
- How long should my child's lessons be?
- Does my child have to practice during the holidays?
- How can I tell if my child has musical aptitude? (Or none whatsoever!)
- My child is 15 — is it too late to start?

• Should I become heavily involved in these lessons, or give my child space when they are working?

• Which instruments are going to help my child most if they want to be involved in the band program at school?

• Am I better off choosing a teacher with a small studio, or a multi-studio complex? What are the advantages/disadvantages of either?

You'll think of plenty of others—the idea is to anticipate questions long before you need to deal with them publicly, and to have *prepared* the answers. It's time well spent. The best way to sound as though you know what you are talking about...is to know what you're talking about.

In other words, no matter how comfortable you are speaking off the cuff, prepare this one.

That having been said, no matter how long your list, you won't be able to anticipate ALL questions. There are some weird parents out there, but be reassured when those weird parents ask their weird question, the rest of the room will perceive it as a weird question too. In other words, you won't lose any points with your audience for not knowing what sort of original period Baroque instruments are best suited to left-handed people, or what sort of link exists between diet and good intonation. Just smile, admit your ignorance on the issue, and move quickly on to the next raised hand.

> **They'll see you in action, recognize that you know what you're talking about, and have an opportunity to actually meet you afterwards.**

Deciding what to include

There's no point in turning your presentation into a three hour epic. Parents are busy, and will be thinking very much about going home after an hour or so. Let them. But this means you have to be smart about what you include in the time you do have.

As you read through your list of anticipated questions, you'll notice some straight away that you already have strong opinions about. You will also see some that you might not be so knowledgeable about, but that are highly likely to be asked. *The answers to those two types of question will make up the body of your presentation* — a combination of information that is most relevant to the audience, and information that you can deliver with the most passion and authority. (Hopefully, quite a few of the questions will actually be in both camps)

> **It's not going to be enough just to put your seminar together. You have to advertise it, or parents will never know it's on in the first place.**

The remaining questions — the more peripheral issues, and questions you know you're not going to be able to speak on at length — you can handle in a less structured Question and Answer session at the end, where shorter answers are more appropriate in any case. Remember, you don't have to answer every question that's put to you. There's no shame in replying "I don't actually know — but if you see me afterwards, I can give you the phone number of somebody who might".

Once you're armed with the content of the seminar, consider begging, borrowing or stealing a laptop, and putting together a PowerPoint presentation. It's very easy to do (even if you've never done it before) and can help focus the audience on key points, while giving them somewhere else in the room to legitimately target their attention, rather than staring at you the whole time.

Advertise your seminar

It's not going to be enough just to put your seminar together. You need to advertise it, or parents will never know it's on in the first place.

Send your local radio station a letter with some of the questions that the seminar will cover — it helps the producer of the show imagine the sorts of questions that the interviewer could ask, and assess whether or not the conversation could be of interest to their listeners. Better still, actually talk to the producer, so that he or she can hear how enthusiastic and knowledgeable you are on the subject.

Write an article for the local paper on "Surviving music lessons", and then ensure that the footnote mentions that you will be giving a free information session for parents who want to learn more.

Put together an information brochure on "How to help your child practice", and leave it at your local music store. Again, make sure that the brochure prominently features the details of your upcoming seminar. (Parents considering music lessons will often visit music stores long before they contact music teachers — as a preliminary costing exercise)

> # Write an article for the local paper on "Surviving music lessons", and then ensure that the footnote mentions your free seminar.

Notify local schools that run in-house instrumental programs — after all, your session should help inspire wavering parents to sign up their kids for music lessons.

Whatever the interest levels from local media, you should also place some ads in your local paper announcing the evening. The added bonus here is that all of this advertising is not just helping to promote the seminar — it's also boosting your own profile in the process.

MASTERCLASS: Be Prepared to Spend

It's not as though every possible promotion tactic will cost money, but many of them do—and some of them will cost a lot. Don't let that put you off. There's a reason that much cleverer business operators than you and I spend until it hurts on advertising every year.

It works.

If you want people to consider your studio, they have to know about it. And if they are to know about it, you have to advertise. Just being a brilliant teacher is not enough, any more than simply having a brilliant new soft drink is enough.

> **The question you need to ask when you find yourself balking at the costs involved is not "Can I afford to", but "Can I afford *not* to".**

You have to budget for the regular and public announcement of your services just as surely as you have to budget for electricity or instrument maintenance.

Coping psychologically with the cost

When you're staring at advertising quotes and shaking your head, one of the things you need to remember is that unlike the acquisition of a whitegood or home entertainment package, it's not dead money once you've spent it. If your advertising campaign is even remotely effective, *you should be earning more from it than you spent on it.* In other words, every dollar you spend should really come back – and with friends.

That's quite independent of the additional non-financial benefits of having a studio with a higher profile.

So the question you always need to ask when you find youself balking at the costs involved is not "Can I afford to", but "Can I afford *not* to".

The very best thing a startup studio can spend their limited resources on is promotion. It's the only thing that in of itself can actually generate fresh students—and therefore fresh income. And if your campaign is well thought out, well targeted, and well implemented, it will pay for itself very, very quickly.

Set aside a percentage of income

One way to lessen the pain of promotion costs is to actually quarantine a proportion of your income, so that you know it cannot be used for any other purpose apart from promotion. That way, your big newspaper ad won't feel like it's robbing you of a new television set—the money was never really yours to spend on a television set in the first place.

> **If your campaign is well thought out, well targeted and well implemented, it will pay for itself very, very quickly.**

There are two ways to do this. You can either put aside a fixed percentage of income, so that every time you bank a check, you transfer an amount into the Promotions account.

Alternatively, you might simply want to regard every Nth student as being there to pay for promotion, so that their entire check goes into that account. It will be up to you to decide what "N" is, but the more you can manage to put aside, the greater the potential impact on future studio growth .

Keep accurate records

Everything you do in the name of studio promotion should be tax deductible, but that's no use to you unless you keep track of the expenses themselves. I'm not just talking about the big ticket items like radio commercials or Yellow Pages here. It's the little things that really add up, and you'll need to keep receipts for all of them—items like stationery, postage stamps, toner cartridges, phone calls. Individually, they may hardly seem worth claiming in the first place, but collectively they can pack a big punch over a twelve month period—the total is often more than some of your Big Ticket promotion expenses.

Talk to your accountant, find out what's deductible and what's not, and then claim everything you're entitled to.

Making the pie bigger

By the time most prospective students are meeting with you, they are already clear that music lessons are a good idea—the only question is which studio they should go to. Which means that the eventual distribution of those students becomes about dividing up the slices of the pie. Your studio will end up with a bigger or smaller slice depending on the effectiveness of your own promotions.

We are competing with hundreds of other potential activities...the list is as long as the Yellow Pages is thick.

There is another way though. Sometimes instead of competing with other studios over who has the biggest piece, *it's smarter to actually increase the size of the pie itself.* In other words to ensure that people who have never considered lessons before are now thinking about it.

This is an idea that will require the co-operation of other studios - and probably is something that your local MTA should be getting behind. So why would they help? It's simple really.

When we try to attract new students, we are not just competing with other instrumental teachers in town. We are competing first of all with hundreds of other potential activities—tennis lessons, gymnastics, art classes, ice skating...the list is as long as the Yellow Pages is thick.

But even more alarmingly, we are competing with *inertia.* In other words, with the possibility that the child may actually *not sign up for anything at all.*

Inertia is by far the most dangerous enemy of all. Unless parents are given compelling reasons, the easiest thing to do is simply to do...nothing. We can look at music lessons next year, they'll say. There's plenty of time.

No there's not. The role of your local MTA is to provide a little ammunition to combat this sense of "maybe...sometimes... perhaps..." from wavering parents. As teachers we all know the benefits of music lessons transcend mere music—it's time parents were informed too.

This ammunition is not going to be propaganda that talks specifically about how great our *own* studios are. Instead, it will focus on the invisible benefits of *all* music lessons. From pianos to piccolos, tubas to triangles.

Information that you can print out and leave with prospective students — or, what the heck — information we can print out and just leave lying around. Wherever. In doctor's surgery waiting rooms. In neighbors' letter boxes. Published in school newsletters. On noticeboards at crèches. Wherever parents are a captive audience.

Winston Churchill once said that a fanatic is someone can't change their mind, and won't change the subject — if you want the music lessons pie to grow, you have to be an incurable music — lesson-fanatic.

The good news is that we don't have to *make up* benefits. They're real, and easy to describe. Parents with children enrolled in music lessons get a *lot* more for their money than just sightreading and a sense of rhythm.

So why are music lessons so great? Whether you decide to put the answer to the question in brochures, posters, a radio advertising campaign or newspaper ads, you need to be clear on the benefits. And if you want parents to actually pay attention to the message, the answers need to be something they haven't heard before.

Here's what you can tell them.

Training children to cope with *pressure*

"Pressure" is a word which seems to be attached mostly to sports heroes. Making the shot after the final buzzer. Positioning yourself to catch a ball that has been hit high into the glare of the floodlights, while seventy thousand fans at the ground hold their breath, and the remaining forty thousand are willing you to trip on your own shoelaces.

In itself, pressure is actually neutral — it's inherently neither good nor ill. It is simply a logical consequence of caring deeply about the outcome of a situation, while simultaneously being in a position where *your actions can directly determine that outcome.* Sports analogies are useful because they are the most tangible illustrations, but all adults know that pressure is a regular part of our professional lives, no matter what career we follow.

Music students are in the unusual position of having to confront pressure at an early age, and having to confront it often.

> # We're not merely music teachers.
>
> # We conduct weekly workshops in Dealing with Pressure, and the skills we teach last for life.

And despite the encouragement we are given to *reduce* stress in our lives, this early exposure to pressure is actually a priceless advantage.

Why? It means that when these music students are adults, pressure will feel like a familiar sparring partner, rather than a terrifying Portent of Doom. They will have faced it — and defeated it — in countless exams, concerts, workshops and lessons. They learn to have it work *for* them, rather than sabotaging their best. And they learn to accept it as a natural part of doing things that matter.

Our music lessons won't immunize them from being nervous at an important job interview or presentation. But the skills they acquired in working with nerves for their various music performances are *transferable* — control your breathing, frame the situation positively, focus on the job at hand rather than the consequences. And don't go too fast.

So we are not merely music teachers. We conduct weekly workshops in Dealing with Pressure, and the skills we teach last for life.

How many parents in your neighborhood know this? And how excited about music lessons would they be if they did?

Training children to deal with *criticism*

Despite music teachers' focus on the positives, music lessons are often largely about reshaping things that are *not* working so well.

This means we have to tell it like it is sometimes. Your dynamics are flat. The presto section is simply not fast enough yet.

Your pedalling stinks and I don't think you have ever checked the fingering in that passage on page two.

And the toughest calls of all?

"The idea you have spent so much time on for the development section of the Brahms Sonata simply doesn't work. Here's why. And don't pull that face at me, I've been doing this for a long time, you have to trust me here."

The end result is that music students learn at an early age to regularly accept advice and feedback from people more knowledgeable than themselves. They experience first hand the value of implementing that advice, and come back each week ready for more.

In so doing, they learn the power of an age-old combination for self improvement—hard work, and acting on the counsel of a mentor.

> **They learn the power of an age-old recipe for self improvement—hard work, and acting on the counsel of a mentor.**

It is sad, but plenty of children are not exposed to this process in the normal course of growing up—not through any shortcoming of the parents, but because having a mentor who supervises the development of a new skill does not just *happen*. Parents have to sign up for it. It probably doesn't matter whether it is music lessons, or chess training, or gymnastics, but it has to be *something*.

Why is the process so valuable? It produces adults who are more willing to consider the views of those around them, and who will know when to wisely defer to those who have demonstrated a greater mastery of the subject at hand. They will consult more often, refine their ideas based on trusted feedback from others, and produce better results.

In eight years of lessons, music students would have had their work under scrutiny—and, if a lack of preparation warrants it, under *attack*—on over three *hundred* occasions. One-on-one, so there is no way of sidestepping the criticisms. The positive impact of this goes beyond mere sixteenth notes, and stays with them permanently.

How many parents in your neighborhood know this? And how excited about music lessons would they be if they did?

Training children to *work* - even when they don't feel like it

Much has been made of the excellent academic results that many music students achieve. The often talked about "Mozart Effect" may be responsible, but there is almost certainly another contributing factor.

Music students have a LOT of preparation to get through in order to be ready for an exam or recital. The traditional half an hour a day is actually *three and a half hours* a week (!). The thing to keep in mind is that there is no way any student will feel like doing that amount of practice *all* the time.

But with the Big Day drawing ever closer, *most of them actually do the work anyway.* The reasons may not be noble — fear of making a complete goose of themselves is often a big motivating factor for getting the work done — but somewhere, somehow, a lot of work goes on that the student probably does not feel like doing. The evidence for this is that despite all our gripes about pupils who don't practice, most of our students end up ready for their performances most of the time. (Stop yelling at the book and think about it for a second! The performance disasters are the *exceptions*, not the rule, so, logically, not being prepared must also be the exception.)

At school, projects, quizzes and mid term papers are just other performances to get ready for. They won't feel like working on those either.

But as their music teacher, you will have helped them confront the reality that you just Do It Anyway. It's a message that certainly won't bring any protests from parents.

How many parents in your neighbourhood know this? And how excited about music lessons would they be if they did?

Coping gracefully with the referee's decision

It's happened to all of us at some time. A student has got up, played better than they ever have before… only to be buried by the thoughtless clod who was adjudicating. Similar to the examiner last year who gave them a B- when they deserved an A+.

Music is a subjective game, and the umpire's decision can be a little bewildering sometimes. But music students eventually learn to live with it, and accept the good calls with the bad.

Why? Because sooner or later, they will receive an A+ when they deserved a B-, and nature will balance itself. And in the transparent absurdity of that outcome will be the realization that a referee's decision is not Truth or Reality. It is an opinion, from a person, and is both fallible and transient.

> **Music is a subjective game, and the umpire's decision can be a little bewildering sometimes.**

They will still read carefully the piece of paper that tells them why they weren't even placed in that flute competition, but they won't allow such bad news to depress them in any sort of life-changing way.

The first time they are passed over for a promotion at work, they will think of the rotten adjudicators they have had over the years, and realize that they may simply be in the presence of another.

But they will also read the feedback on their job performance appraisal carefully — because their years of music lessons have also trained them to do just that — just to see if there is anything they can do better next time.

Philosophical about the outcome, proactive about the accompanying criticisms. Sounds like a healthy and constructive way to deal with disappointment, and it will sound that way to a lot of the parents in your studio too.

How many parents in your neighbourhood know this? And how excited about music lessons would they be if they did?

Getting back on the horse

If you give enough performances, sooner or later you will have a disaster. A memory lapse that brings the whole recital crashing down around your ears. Forgetting to take a repeat that the rest of the ensemble observes, and then getting hopelessly lost. Starting too fast, and having the presto section skid, and then disintegrate into a thousand smouldering sixteenth notes. Ouch.

(Go on. I bet you can picture three such performances that *you* have given at some stage. I have trouble limiting my mental list to only three!)

The real battle actually starts not at the performance itself, but in those weeks afterwards. How will the student react? And more importantly, how do you get them to pick themselves up, dust themselves off, and focus on the next concert?

Performances end up being metaphors for countless situations music students will face in their later life, and they will experience the same mixture of triumphs and setbacks that we all do.

> **By the time they have completed a decade of music lessons, they will have had to bounce back from plenty of disappointments...**
>
> **...and they will become better equipped adults because of it.**

By the time they have completed a decade of music lessons, they will have had to bounce back from plenty of disappointments. But they'll also have experienced many more successes, helping them to get a snapshot of a valuable big picture that has become a cliché that few adults truly understand:

The important thing is not that they fell, but how quickly they got back on the horse.

Taking this metaphor absolutely as far as we can, because music students ride more than just about any other kids, they will have had plenty of practice at dealing constructively with being thrown. And they will become better equipped adults because of it.

How many parents in your neighbourhood know this? And how excited about music lessons would they be if they did?

Project management, and coping with deadlines

Much has been made of the two basic realities of life being death and taxes, but there is actually a third Unavoidable. *Deadlines.*

There are two types of deadline that music students become very experienced at coping with:

1) The Long Term Campaign

An exam or a major recital doesn't just *happen*. They are often first planned a year or more before the actual date.

Pieces are chosen, mini deadlines are set, and a strategy for getting it all done in time is established. Quality control checkpoints are built in along the way in the form of mock exams and workshops.

The end result? Very young students are able to build quite epic events one small step at a time, and become used to the idea that what they do today prepares them for tomorrow — and sometimes for a tomorrow that is actually twelve months away.

I don't think I need to list some non-musical examples of how this will help them later, and it makes a lie of the notion that kids are only ever focussed on short-term gratification.

2) The High-Pressure short term deadline

No chance to mount a steady campaign for this type of deadline. Instead, it's a case of take a deep breath, put your head down, and swim like a lunatic until you get to the finish line. These are the short-notice concerts, the performances they suddenly have to give at school, or the filling in for someone who has unexpectedly fallen ill.

If a manager needs to look around for someone who will cope with a sudden burst of intense work, and a ridiculously short deadline, they could do a lot worse than ask each staff member how many years of music lessons they have had.

How many parents in your neighbourhood know this? And how excited about music lessons would they be if they did?

Developing many gears of focus

Whenever I hear someone say that children cannot concentrate, I want to strap them down and make them watch a student recital.

In the course of even a short piece the child will have to closely supervise hundreds of individual decisions: Which note comes next? How loud should I be playing? How can I recover from that little slip I just made? How staccato should the middle section be? How long should I hold this fermata before moving on to the next note? Have I already done the repeat or not? How can I improve my intonation right now?

> **It can be quite moving to watch, and makes you wonder what else these children would be capable of.**

The room is silent, all attention is focussed on them, and all *their* attention is focussed on the moment. It can be quite moving to watch, and makes you wonder what else these children would be capable of.

But what is most exciting is that the concentration exhibited in the performance itself is actually just the tip of a much larger iceberg. For this performance to occur at all, the same child had to be still and focussed in dozens of lessons and hundreds of practice sessions. The audience never gets to see these, but we are talking about many, many hours of intense application that would not have happened without music lessons.

They also become used to the idea that focus *comes in different gears.* It's not as though they have to be concentrating until the veins stand out on their neck all the time. There will be moments in the lesson in which they can joke about what happened on the weekend, and others where they will need every last reserve of focus. This ratio will gently shift as the Big Day nears.

So it's not just that they know how to focus—they also learn *when.* This helps ensure that they can not only deliver their best when it's needed, but that they don't turn themselves into stresspots in the process.

How many parents in your neighbourhood know this? And how excited about music lessons would they be if they did?

Learning the power of positive assumptions

As teachers, we have all learned the hard way of the very real link between a student's assumption about how a performance is *likely* to go, and then what *actually* happens on the Big Day.

In fact, the impact of positive thinking is so powerful that it can help pull an otherwise underprepared student through a performance. Conversely, the *absence* of such thinking can turn performances of even well-prepared students into a hopeless mush of otherwise undeserved errors.

Because of this, much of our teaching in the final weeks before the performance is spent helping students be in the right frame of mind. We reassure. We praise. We walk them through the whole thing, and paint the performance as a triumph long before the first notes are played.

Granted, there are plenty of other activities where children can experience for themselves the tangible impact of projection. But there are none quite so immediately telling as what happens to you when you think such thoughts—good or ill—in front of an *audience*.

On the various Big Occasions that they have throughout the rest of their life, your music students will not only be well versed in the importance of positive thinking, but they will be equipped with the strategies to ensure that it happens at the right time.

How many parents in your neighbourhood know this? And how excited about music lessons would they be if they did?

Learning that progress is not always linear

...which is just a fancy way of saying that we don't always improve at a constant rate. But it's an essential lesson to learn as early as possible.

How does it play itself out in music lessons? Some months will feel like Golden Ages, where the student will pick up new ideas with ease, and where the notes will fall well for them every time they play. They'll get more done in fifteen minutes of practice than they would normally achieve in a few days.

Two months later, and they are struggling a little, the Midas touch having deserted them as they plod from lesson to lesson.

The idea that some months will be better than others is not a new concept for most students. In fact they are probably even ready to embrace the flip-side idea that for this to be possible, at other times progress will have to be slower. (By definition, this HAS to happen!)

> **When we teach a child how to play a musical instrument, we are showing them how to become good at *something*.**
>
> **This is the greatest gift of music lessons.**

What comes as a shock is that sometimes they will actually go *backwards*. Weeks so unproductive that they are sure that their playing was in better shape a couple of months ago.

"Backward" progress not only ok, it's actually quite normal. Even within a practice session, there can be a ten minute block where everything the student attempts goes wrong. Why would there not be days or even weeks where the stars feel similarly badly aligned, or where St. Cecilia frowns upon everything you do?

It's not really a backward step — it's just an inevitable part of long term progress. But it sure as heck *feels* like a backward step, and that's where the danger resides.

People who don't have the opportunity to learn this lesson early can sometimes become so discouraged at the first appearance of a backward step that they mark down the activity as too hard, and give up completely. In equipping our students with an awareness of the likelihood of occasional backward steps, we are not only steeling their resolve for music lessons, we are toughening them for hundreds of other activities that they haven't even met yet.

How many parents in your neighbourhood know this? And how excited about music lessons would they be if they did?

The greatest benefit of all

Most of our students are not destined to become concert artists. (Most of their parents are not hoping they will be either!)

When we teach a child how to play a musical instrument, we are showing them how to become good at *something*. This is the greatest gift of music lessons.

Most of the advice we give for them to achieve this has little to do with music itself. Break big jobs into little jobs. Start early if you have a big project to undertake. Stay calm and focussed under pressure. Analyze your own work for weaknesses and then target the things that aren't so strong. Persist in the face of difficulties. Allocate the time that the job requires. Work whether you feel like it or not. Listen to your teacher, and respect your peers.

And enjoy what you do, for none of it is worth pursuing unless it makes you smile from time to time.

They may not end up being concert artists, but these children can apply these skills to just about anything that they want to end up being good at.

Our true reward?

In the doctors and sculptors, the ice skaters, plumbers, poets and chefs of tomorrow, we can claim forever a part in their success that was their music lessons.

This is not just rhetoric. As music teachers, we change the lives of the people we work with.

Go find some like-minded teachers at your MTA, and start to spread the word. Some of the most enthusiastic additions to any studio are not those who were always going to have music lessons, but those who, until recently, were not even contemplating it.

If this section has been useful for you, and you would like to include quotes in your own propaganda, there's an online version available at the "For Teachers" section of the PracticeSpot website at:

http://www.practicespot.com/article.phtml?id=111

Create a competition...with a twist

Music competitions end up generating a lot of attention. We ought to know — as teachers we end up *paying* them a lot of attention. There are rules to consider, forms to submit, adjudications to read through, students to prepare and parents to keep updated. And that's to say nothing of the excitement that is created by the day itself.

Even once the event has been and gone, competitions leave a lingering mark in the form of the certificates that sit on students' fridges, and the countless "here's what we'll do differently next time" consolation speeches to those who returned ribbonless. Like a carnival, they create anticipation, change the town for a day when they're here, and then leave plenty of memories afterwards.

> **You don't just want to be a *consumer* of competitions.**
>
> **If you really want to get people talking about your studio, you should *create* one.**

Which is why you don't just want to be a *consumer* of competitions.

If you really want to get people talking about your studio, you should *create* one.

It's a lot of work, but being known as the creative and enthusiastic person who invented, organized and ran a successful competition will speak volumes for your teaching, long before any interview takes place. And being *your* competition, it can feature the name of your studio prominently, meaning that any advertising for the event itself also doubles as advertising for your studio.

Some ideas...

You don't have to set up a major international Grand Prix de Musique for this to be a success both as a competition, and as a promotion device. But if you want other studios to pay attention to your competition, then you need to make sure that it offers something...different.

In fact, the aim should be to ensure that the only way students can experience an event like it is to actually take part in yours.

So what sorts of competition might capture their attention? You'll think of plenty of ideas of your own, but some suggestions are below:

Short preparation championship:

There are plenty of competitions out there that give students months to prepare, together with some at the other end of the spectrum that focus on sight reading. But there's nothing in between.

You would need a space with a dozen small rehearsal rooms. The idea is that the participants are given the music an hour before the performance begins, and are free to spend the hour practicing however they would like. It's not sight reading, as students do genuinely have the chance to rehearse the tricky bits. But the sixty minute limit means that only students with highly efficient practice techniques will prevail.

The advantage to participants? Some of the students who are always being beaten in conventional eisteddfods, and don't rate themselves highly as sightreaders will come into their own. And you can pair it up with a workshop on practicing, with a range of local teachers each contributing a session.

Great undiscovered gems:

Participants can play whatever they like, but it must be composers and/or works that nobody has heard of before. They don't have to be little known *contemporary* composers (although they are probably the easiest to find) — there are plenty of baroque and classical composers who also languish in obscurity.

The focus is not on who gives the best performances, but on who discovers the best *pieces*. Teachers will go along partly to support their own students, but mostly to pick up new ideas for repertoire.

Jekyll and Hyde festival:

To help students think outside the interpretation square. Each participant has to play their selected work not once, but *twice* in a row—but the aim is to produce two completely different interpretations of the same work. Different tempi, different dynamic decisions, different treatment of rubato, different tone—the more radical the difference the better.

Good taste will occasionally be a casualty, but merely participating should shatter forever a student's belief that there is only one way to play a piece. And as teachers, we'll be reminded again of what's possible when the imaginations of students are unshackled.

> **The aim is to produce two completely different interpretations of the same work.**
>
> **As teachers, we'll be reminded again of what's possible when the imaginations of students are unshackled.**

A Scales Bee:

Similar to a spelling bee, except that participants are called forward to deliver scales of the moderator's choosing. Like a spelling bee, it's sudden death—the first flat where a sharp should go, or missed fingering, and the student is out.

And also like a spelling bee, the scales start off easy, and get progressively nastier. So in the early stages, a pianist might simply be asked to play one octave of G Major with their right hand.

By the end, the last couple of competitors will be fighting it out as they play Ab melodic minor in triplets in their left hand (3 octaves) at the same time as they play B Major in sixteenth notes in their right hand (4 octaves), contrary motion of course.

A panel of teachers can have a lot of fun coming up with the scales challenges that lie between those two extremes.

Great openings:

Starting a piece can be the most dangerous time of all for a lot of students, which is what makes this particular challenge so irresistible. Instead of delivering complete works, competitors will play the first eight bars from a dozen different pieces. Their job? To make the excerpts arresting, and in character from the very first note. Ten second pause between each, but no time to settle otherwise.

Successful students will have to show a remarkable presence of mind, together with a thorough understanding of the spirit of the opening of each work. But not only that, all candidates will emerge from the exercise with a better understanding of what makes an opening sink or swim—after all, in the course of the afternoon, they will have heard hundreds of them.

> **Instead of delivering complete works, competitors will play the first eight bars from a dozen different pieces.**

Again, it's worth backing this up with a workshop where colleagues can brainstorm with students the elements that go to making openings commanding.

Peer Review:

No adjudicators in this one, no prizes either, but more feedback than a student has ever had before. And this time it's from a source that they can't ignore — their fellow students.

The idea is that when students are not actually performing, they will be in the audience, armed with pencil and paper. Their job is to write comments about what they just heard.

At the end of each performance, the pieces of paper are gathered up and given to the teacher, making fertile ground for discussions next lesson. (And also giving the teacher a chance to word some of the criticisms a little more tactfully before passing them on!)

The student would also create their own report of their own performance, and it's always interesting to see how closely their perception is matched by those who heard them play. That memory lapse they had towards the end might not feel so bad if none of the other students actually picked up on it.

To help students write comments, it's a good idea to make them Specialists — in other words for each student to have one particular musical element that they are responsible for assessing. So there will be a student whose job it is to assess the steadiness of the tempo. Another will be listening for dynamics. Another might be focused on intonation. Yet another might simply be assessing how the performer carried themselves on and off the stage.

> **No adjudicators in this one, no prizes either, but more feedback than a student has ever had before.**
>
> **And this time it's from a source that they can't ignore— their fellow students.**

In this way, the performer gets a comprehensive picture of the entire performance through feedback on dozens of individual elements.

But the most important benefit flows not from receiving the feedback, but from *giving* it. For many students it will be the first time that their opinion has been sought in this fashion, and it lays the groundwork for being able to give better self assessments in the future.

Getting the logistics right

Once you've decided what sort of competition to create, the real work begins. The first thing you should do is track down some existing competition organizers and spend half an hour chatting to them — they'll have all sorts of advice that should make your job easier. The list below is by no means comprehensive, but are all things that you should think about:

Venue

Most of the costs will be associated with venue hire, so it pays to spend some time finding the right place. You also need to ensure that toilet facilities are available, together with tea and coffee making if you are providing refreshments.

If you have been supportive of and are well known to your local school, this might be a time that they can help, by providing low or no cost hall hire

Sponsorship

Once the details for the competition are firm, approach some local businesses about sponsorship. Come to them pre-armed with several levels of sponsorship—from small ads that might appear in programs, right through to banners that hang behind the performers, or the opportunity to make presentations to the winners.

In return, they might help pay for some of the competition costs, or supply prizes.

Competition brochure

This document needs to not only announce the competition, but spell out conditions of entry, outline any prizes, and provide all the "where, when and how" information that teachers would need, together with any advertising from sponsors. This brochure is designed both for other teachers to read, and to be a document they can hand out to their students.

Entry Form

This is what would-be competitors send back to you to be enrolled. The form would contain fields for all the information you would need from a student, together with clear details about the deadline for submitting the form, and any associated costs and acceptable methods of payment.

Adjudicators/panellists/presenters:

You need to make the approach long before the competition starts, and then make a small stipend available for their time. Make sure you have thank you notes and gifts to present at the conclusion of the competition.

Publicity

Your competition will start to work for you as a studio promotion tool long before the competition itself starts. The best thing you can do—both for the competition and your own studio—is to advertise it as well and as widely as you can. Take out a newspaper ad, contact your local radio stations, hand out brochures at your next MTA meeting, talk to the arts editor of your local paper, ask for 90 seconds at the end of other studio recitals to promote the competition itself, have your students put up posters in shop windows, have your sponsors give out information to customers...if you want this to be a blazing success, then you need to hype it.

> **Your competition will start to work for you as a studio promotion tool long before the competition itself starts.**

Participation Fee

Competitions can involve significant setup costs, but ideally, the participants should cover it all. The participation fee shouldn't just be a nice round number—it needs to be carefully worked out based on how many entrants you are expecting, together with the total cost of the competition itself.

All of this looks like a lot of work because it *is* a lot of work. But that's part of what makes a competition such a great flagship for your studio. The assumption in parents' minds will be that if you have the enterprise, creativity and organising skills to make a competition like this a success, what could you do for their child in weekly lessons?

As soon as that question starts being asked, every second you have spent on the competition will have been worthwhile.

Newspaper Advertising

Newspaper ads have the capacity to make your phone ring, but you have to be smart about how and when you use them. The most tempting thing to do is simply to put a couple of lines in the classifieds — because it's cheap.

Don't. As soon as parents see:

```
Flute Lessons. Call 5542-8334.
Exp. teacher, gd. rates
```

they will assume all sorts of things that you don't want them to assume.

> **If your advertisement looks cheap, parents will assume all sorts of things that you don't want them to assume.**

• That because the ad is so short, and that you have also resorted to abbreviating words means that you obviously can only afford a cheap ad. Which means your studio can't be doing very well. Which means you're probably not a very good teacher.

• For "gd. rates" to be fully half of the features you mention means that as far as your concerned, price is one of your best features. Which means your other features can't be very exciting.

• The ad itself smacks of you not having very many students, and being desperate for more. Which means that you can't be very good at attracting students in the first place, or keeping those that do come aboard. Readers will be wondering why.

• Your ad will be sitting alongside plenty of other similarly worded ads for music lessons, meaning that there is nothing to differentiate you from your competition. Which means that your studio can't be anything special.

All of this means that your phone is probably not going to ring.

But it would probably be worse if it *did*. Because an ad like that is really only going to be of interest to a parent who:

1) Is not interested to know any details about a teacher before they approach them

2) Thinks that "gd. rates" is a big plus in a teacher for their child

You don't want parents with priorities like that in your studio, because they are not going to appreciate what you're going to offer in the first place, are unlikely to be providing their child with much support between lessons, and are probably going to resist purchasing the resources that their child really needs—which means second rate instruments, saying "no" to workshops that have fees attached, and pressuring you for photocopies rather than buying new books.

So how do you get around this problem?

Two ways. Your first option is to create a classified ad that is going to stand out from the crowd, and communicate more effectively just what makes your studio worthwhile.

Your second option is to spend the same money you would have spent on dozens of classified ads, and spend it on a single display ad instead.

Classifieds: sneaky tricks

Despite the warnings above, classifieds do have two advantages that make them worth considering:

• They are relatively inexpensive, and can be made cheaper still if multiple weeks are purchased. This takes the pressure off any individual ad—if your listing is ignored completely one week, it won't have cost you that much. (Whereas if a large display ad is ignored completely, all you can do is mumble something about "at least it's a tax deduction" as you kiss goodbye to hundreds of dollars)

• Similar to Yellow Pages ads, classifieds are an example of *indexed* advertising, meaning that parents who are actively seeking music lessons will be searching in the same place that your ad is. You don't have to hope that they will just happen to stumble across it while browsing articles.

By themselves, these advantages will not offset the dangers outlined at the start of this section. To make your classified work for you, rather than against you, there are a number of things to check:

> **To make your classified work for you, rather than against you, there are a number of things to check.**

Ensuring your ad stands out visually

Your ad won't be the only one in the section for "Music Tuition", but you want to ensure that it is the only one that people see at a first glance. Given that you normally cannot include any graphics in the ad, you have to be clever with your text options.

Remember, your ad can normally include any alphanumeric symbol, together with additional "glyphs" that you might normally only be able to access on your keyboard by hitting "SHIFT" while you hold a number — e.g.. $!@#%^&*()$, or by choosing "insert symbol" from your word processor. By using these, you can ensure that your ad has an eye-catching border — the example below simply uses the "tilde" symbol alternating with a bullet point, but you'll come up with your own combinations:

~•~•~•~•~•~•~•~•~•~•~•~•~•~
MARCIA'S FLUTE STUDIO
Hightown's beginner specialist
First 2 lessons free. 9965-4432
~•~•~•~•~•~•~•~•~•~•~•~•~•~

You won't win any awards for graphic design, but that's not the aim—all you are trying to do is ensure that your ad does not fade into the background. The border is simply there to create a feeling of "this one is not like the others."

Another trick is to actually have a *completely blank* first and last line. You will still be charged for those two lines, but it will ensure that there is something...different...about your ad. Which is exactly what you want. In a page full of ads that all start and end with text, a reader's eyes will be drawn by yours, simply because it doesn't blend into the crowd.

Ensuring your *content* is memorable

Having ensured that your ad is likely to be looked at, you then need to ensure that the message itself is worthy of that attention—otherwise the reader will quickly move on to the next most eye-catching ad.

> **WIth only a couple of lines to play with, you're not going to be able to give a comprehensive summary of all that your studio offers.**

With only a couple of lines to play with, you're not going to be able to give a comprehensive summary of all that your studio offers. One powerful way to get around this is to use one of the lines giving the address of your studio webpage (see p 218 for details on how to set up a free one instantly). Not only will the very fact that you have a studio web presence in the first place make your studio seem professional and established, but the webpage itself can be packed with details that your classified ad never could contain:

∧∧*∧*∧*∧*∧*∧*∧*∧
STAWELL MUSIC CENTER
Professional, creative piano lessons
www.stawell.practicespot.com
7754-8897 for free interview
∧∧*∧*∧*∧*∧*∧*∧*∧*

Consider an ad that's not an ad

Instead of simply posting a slogan, a phone number, and a web address, you might want to consider using the space simply to congratulate a student:

> ✻∧✻∧✻∧✻∧✻∧✻∧✻∧✻∧✻∧
> **STUDENT OF THE WEEK!**
> Lisa ROBERTS—for great practice
> Stawell Music Center 7754 8897
> www.stawell.practicespot.com
> ✻∧✻∧✻∧✻∧✻∧✻∧✻∧✻∧✻∧✻

This ad achieves a number of things with six short lines.

• It tells parents that your studio rewards students for good work — and will go to some trouble to do so.

• It will absolutely make Lisa's week! (Everyone loves to be mentioned in the paper), and will have the rest of your students wondering what they can do to receive a similar public accolade.

• It will almost certainly be the only "Congratulations" message that appears in the section, helping ensure that it stands out.

• And it also provides the essential information that the other ads do, together with a link to your website (which the other ads probably don't)

That's a lot of value from six lines of advertising. As for any advertisement, you would need to track the results (See p 214), but don't be surprised if enquiries follow.

Place several contrasting ads in the one section

If you want to completely dominate a listing, you should consider submitting more than one ad. The idea would be to create three or four different ads for the one classified section, each highlighting a different aspect of why your studio is so great.

Examples are below

~•~•~•~•~•~•~•~•~•~•~•~•~•~
STAWELL MUSIC CENTER
Professional, creative piano lessons
7754-8897 for free interview
~•~•~•~•~•~•~•~•~•~•~•~•~•~

•~•~•~•~•~•~•~•~•~•~•~•~•~•~
PIANO & KEYBOARD LESSONS
Stawell Music Center — est. 15 yrs
www.stawell.practicespot.com
~•~•~•~•~•~•~•~•~•~•~•~•~•~

•~•~•~•~•~•~•~•~•~•~•~•~•~
TWO FREE PIANO LESSONS...
It's time. Discover your music.
Stawell Music Center 7754 — 8897
•~•~•~•~•~•~•~•~•~•~•~•~•~

Obviously cost may prevent you from being able to do this as often as a single listing, but sometimes the impact of several in one week can exceed that of one ad that runs over several weeks. As with all the other promotion techniques, try it, track it, and make adjustments based on the results.

Display ads

These ads will appear somewhere in the body of the newspaper itself, and will be a lot bigger and more expensive than the classified option.

So what do you get for your extra money?

• The extra space is not just a question of bigger being better. It means that you can include *details* about your studio, rather than having to reduce everything you offer into a six word slogan.

These details will help your studio feel more "real" to prospective parents, as well as being a powerful vehicle for creating a sense of what's unique about your tuition.

• While the classifieds will feature plenty of other teachers, chances are that you are probably the only music teacher to take out a full display ad. And I'm not just talking about that issue of the newspaper. You probably would be the first music teacher to take such a step for the past six months.

You can include details about your studio, rather than having to reduce everything you do to a six word slogan.

This creates an instant competitive edge for you as soon as someone sees the ad—not only will your studio be noticed, but others will be conspicuous by their absence.

• Such an ad will give you exposure to parents who are *passively* rather than actively seeking music lessons. Such parents won't be hunting through the "music tuition" section of the classifieds yet, but should be interested enough to stop and read a music teacher advertisement ad should they happen to stumble on one. And the fact that it's a big one they stumbled on won't hurt at all.

• Display ads will also create the impression that your studio must be doing well—the expectation is that music teachers would typically only advertise in the classifieds, and so your display ad is a sign that your studio is thriving. As discussed at the beginning of the book, your studio might not be thriving at all, but as long as your Lobby appears to be the gateway to a bustling and successful studio, then it will be perceived that way by prospective students.

Being smart about the timing

Because they are relatively inexpensive, classified ads can be lines in the water on dozens of occasions for you during the year — in fact, many teachers will take advantage of the bulk rates that come with having a whole year of weekly classifieds.

Yellow Pages ads can cost hundreds or thousands of dollars, but again can work for you every day of the year. Your display ad is a different story. Weighing in at hundreds of dollars, *and vanishing the day after the ad appears*, the timing of your display ad has to be handled carefully.

You want to ensure that the ad goes in when:

1) The greatest number of prospective students is likely to be reading the paper. It's no good scheduling your ad for a long weekend, when a lot of families might be taking a short holiday.

> **Weighing in at hundreds of dollars, and vanishing the day after the ad appears, the timing of your display ad has to be handled carefully.**

2) At a time of the year when most parents are actually thinking about starting music lessons. Which means that an ad in the middle of a busy school semester is not the best idea. Parents and students will be flat out just trying to keep up with what they're already doing, and are probably not entertaining the idea of even more commitments.

The best time to catch families is *just before the school year starts,* or even in that very first week of school. That's often when the big decisions will be made about the year ahead — it's close enough to school time to feel relevant, but far enough away from the madness of having to do it all that lessons will feel possible.

170

Being smart about *which publication* features your ad

It's no good putting your ad in Kickboxing Monthly, or the Rural Times. The readership does not need to be exclusively parents with young families, but that demographic should be well represented.

But that's only half the story. Your ad may well be read enthusiastically by thousands of parents who are desperate for music lessons — but if they live an hour's car trip away, then it's not going to help your phone ring. So when the advertising staff are dazzling you with distribution figures, make sure you ask for statistics that are specific to the area in which you live.

All other things being equal, the most likely candidates for students are still those that share your zip code. With every city block added between you and the reader, the chances of an enquiry diminishes, no matter how slick your ad might be.

Being smart about *where* the ad appears

Depending on the paper, you should have some control over where the ad appears. It's not as though you will be able to specify "Top of page 12, left hand corner, 2 inches from the margin", but you should be able to nominate which section of the paper.

It then becomes a question of trying to second-guess where prospective students are most likely to browse. Because the interests of students can be so diverse, this can be tough to pin down — but if the paper features a "For Parents" magazine, that will be a better bet than a page dedicated to horse-racing results.

The best thing to do is to put the question to the advertising section of the paper. They should have information available about the demographic of the readership of each of the sections of their paper, and should be able to steer you towards the most effective placement.

Being smart about how the ad *looks*

Unlike the classified ads with the do-it-yourself borders, this display ad *has* to look slick. This means that unless you have specialized layout software (Quark, Pagemaker, Indesign for example), and the skills to use it, you should put the design of the ad in the hands of someone who knows what they are doing. By their very nature, display ads tend to yell "Hey! Look at me!" — once you have that attention, the ad has to look good.

First of all try to track down a friend or family member who might be able to help you out. Alternatively, the newspaper itself will usually offer layout services for an extra fee — it's worth it. If you're really serious about your ad having maximum impact, a dedicated graphic design business can produce even better results, but can actually double the cost of your ad. Again, before being put off by such costs, consider how many students it would take to pay for the exercise, and balance that against how many enquiries such a professional looking ad might generate.

> **Before being put off by the costs, consider how many students it would take to pay for the exercise...**
>
> **...and balance that against how many enquiries a professional looking ad might generate.**

Remember, this ad won't just be seen by prospective students. It will be seen by existing students, colleagues, and current and future strategic partners. You want an ad that you can be proud of — the impact will actually remain long after the ad physically disappears. And should you ever want to run the same display ad again, the second time around, there would be no design fees.

Make it look like news

Once the ad has been noticed, it's more likely to be actually *read* if it seems to contain useful information. So instead of simply just headlining with the name of your studio, consider leading with an **announcement** of some sort.

"Important announcement for flute students"

"The secret behind Stawell's most creative music lessons"

"Stawell Flute Studio: interviewing new students now"

"Stawell Flute Studio Practice-a-thon coming soon"

Alternatively, you could use the space to give a few short **tips** on an issue that might be of interest to parents considering music lesson — or better still, something that might help parents consider music lessons for the very first time.

"The best way to get your child into a school band"

"Music lessons: why they give your child the edge"

"The parent's role in music lessons"

Not only are parents more likely to actually read your copy (because it's potentially useful for them), but the ad will stamp you immediately as an expert who thinks carefully about what they do — and someone who is likely to offer solutions, not just lessons.

Refer them to your studio webpage for the full story

Despite the extra space that a display ad provides, it still won't be enough for you to describe everything your studio offers. That's where your studio webpage can come to the rescue — all you need to do is put at the bottom of your ad:

"For further information, visit the studio website at..."

Parents who have been impressed by your ad, but are still not sure enough to call, then have an easy way of learning more. Your website will provide them with an email address and phone number if they want to get in touch.

Regardless of whether or not they actually visit your studio website, the very fact that you have one puts you ahead of most other teachers, and creates an "established" feel to your studio. (see p 218 for information on how to set yours up instantly)

Create a shortlist before you layout

With a newspaper display ad likely to be a once-a-year shot, the content is something that you must get right, and the more feedback you can get, the better. Long before you start worrying about laying out your display ad, you should create a few different possibilities for the text, and then run them past some other people. Family, friends, whoever. Ask which of the versions they prefer, and why.

Even if your own instincts are screaming otherwise, if eight of the nine people you approached responded most favorably to Version no. 2, then Version no. 2 it should be.

> **Even if your instincts are screaming otherwise, if eight of the nine people you approached responded most favorably to Version no. 2, then Version no. 2 it should be.**

If your layout process involves having to choose between several possible concepts, you should get feedback on that too. Granted, it's still a small sample, and should not be confused with market research, but it's much more reliable than a sample of *one* – which is exactly what you would be leaping into this with if you don't ask for opinions.

MASTERCLASS: **Repeated Exposure**

While you should certainly be tracking results of your advertising closely, it's important to understand that not all of the campaigns are actually designed to make your phone ring immediately. Many of them are simply about increasing familiarity with your studio's name, so that when the time does come for a potential student to be browsing through the Yellow Pages, you have the most powerful advantage of all:

That they have heard of you already.

Think about it for moment—and don't protest that you would be immune from the power of familiarity in your own purchasing decisions. When you're standing in a supermarket aisle, trying to choose between twenty different brands of yoghurt, you're in a very similar position to parents who are selecting music teachers for the very first time. They don't know much about music. You probably don't know too much about yoghurt.

Which means that in

> **If your phone is not ringing in the first 48 hours after your newspaper ad went in, don't panic.**

the absence of any compelling rational reason to choose one over another, the fact that you can hum the jingle for "Yumolicious Yoghurt! " just might tip the scales to your picking that up at the expense of another brand that you haven't heard of before. The logic is that if something is known to you, it's more trustworthy than something unknown.

This is sometimes referred to as "Brand Awareness", and can be a powerful trigger for choice—especially when the consumer does not have the expertise or information available to assess the products for themselves in any other way. And potential students usually have neither the expertise nor the information available to make genuinely informed choices about music lessons.

Here's what you need to remember:

The time parents first hear about your studio should be long before they are looking for a music teacher. That way, when the moment for choosing a music teacher really does come along, your studio's name will be familiar to them, and you will have the inside running over everyone else.

So if your phone is not ringing in the first 48 hours after your newspaper ad went in, don't panic. Every person who saw the ad—and a lot of people will have—will have stored away your studio name to some extent. And then, in six months time when they are actually seeking music lessons for the first time, they'll see a notice in their letterbox about music lessons with you...and the name will feel somehow...familiar.

> **The time parents first hear about your studio should be long before they are looking for a music teacher.**

In this way, your ads will end up reinforcing each other. A parent who simply sees your poster in a shop window is not necessarily going to give you a call. But if they have also seen a newspaper ad, and your yellow pages ad, seen your name on the sponsor's list for the school play, and noticed that you were the organizer of the music competition that their old teacher took part in, then suddenly the poster won't just look like a name to them. It will be a name they know.

And we trust—and call—names we know.

Ask yourself this right now:

How many different ways can potential students encounter the name of your studio at the moment? How regularly are they likely to encounter each one of them? How many of these ads will they only stumble across once they are actively looking for a music teacher?

If the answers seem a little thin, then it's time to diversify your profile, and take steps to ensure that your existing campaigns are noticed more regularly.

Become a Sponsor

There are plenty of worthwhile endeavours and organizations that can only survive with the support of individual or corporate sponsors. The relationship is symbiotic—the organizations are provided with resources that they need, while the sponsor is given public recognition of their assistance.

The important thing to remember is that this is not a promotion tool available only to Fortune 500 corporations. The next time a local community theater company—or better yet a *children's* theater company—is rehearsing for a new production, contact the organizer and ask how your studio might be able to assist. You might agree to be the rehearsal pianist, or make a financial contribution towards costumes or printing the program.

> **The assumption will be that if your studio can afford to be a "sponsor", then it must be doing very well...**
>
> **...a sponsorship can really give your Lobby a gilt edge.**

Or you might simply agree to assertively promote the production to the dozens of families that come to your studio, or feature an ad for the show at the bottom of your next studio recital program.

How can this help your studio?

In return, there are many ways that the theatre company can help you at little inconvenience and no cost to them. They might agree to allow you to leave a small brochure about your studio on the seats in the auditorium. They might allow you to put up a banner behind the at-the-door ticket sales. They might allow you to put an ad in their program. Or they might simply announce in the program itself that they were grateful for the support of your studio.

With fifteen minutes to kill before the show, and not much else to do, an ad in such a program would be noticed by just about everyone in the audience.

The demographics for this scenario are ideal. Parents who take their kids to community theatre productions are more likely to be rating music as a priority than someone whose only contact with theater was being a tree in their kindergarten play.

Music competitions and eisteddfods provide similarly exciting possibilities, with many of the sections already having acknowledgements that say "This section proudly sponsored by...". You need to ensure that your studio's name features there too. Such sponsorships don't have to cost you a fortune, and go to the most targeted audience of all—*families that are already involved in having music lessons.*

Remember, sponsorship doesn't have to be about you donating money—you can donate your time or skills. Everyone ends up better off for your involvement: you end up with a stronger profile for your studio, and they end up with a better event because of your assistance. The assumption will be that if your studio can afford to be a "sponsor" (which people might imagine cost you hundreds of dollars!), then it must be doing very well. Which means it must be a good studio. A sponsorship can really give your Lobby a gilt edge.

Possible targets

Arts or child related events are probably the most useful targets for sponsorship, and there are plenty of variations:

• **A local school band that is undertaking their first interstate tour.** You provide expert one-on-one coaching to a couple of instrumentalists who are struggling with their parts in the final few weeks. The band director might then agree to include acknowledgements of your efforts in a letter that goes home to parents of band members.

• **Citywide composition competition.** You sponsor one of the prizes, paying for the trophy and engraving. In return, a note about your sponsorship might appear in the program.

• **Local preschool trying to raise funds to renovate their playground.** You put on a special fund-raising concert. They put a special plaque on the new monkey bars.

• **Children's hospital.** You run a special annual practice-a-thon, proceeds of which all go to the hospital itself. In return, an ad for your studio would be displayed in the elevators at the hospital for six months.

> ## Sponsorship doesn't have to be about you donating money—you can donate your time or skills.

• **Drug awareness event.** Next time there is a "Say no to drugs" day in your town, you might want to ensure that your studio organizes a series of *"Performing. It's the only high you need"* concerts. Liaise with both the Mayor and one of the concert halls in town, and create an event in which hundreds of different children get a chance to perform on a stage that is normally reserved for the city's Symphony orchestra and visiting international artists.

Handled well, it could be one of the major events of the day, and therefore of interest to the media — and if your studio's name is prominent in the creation of the event, don't be surprised when it features prominently in the story.

Keep your eyes open

There are sponsorship opportunities all around you, but they're not going to come knocking on your studio door. *You have to go and find them,* which means you need to be actively looking for candidate events. Keep an eye on the newspaper — most of these events generate a buzz well in advance of the Big Day itself.

Once you've found worthwhile targets, remember that the organizers will be busy people, so you'll need to ensure your idea is completely worked out before you make the approach. And if they're not interested? Try somewhere else — it's their loss.

Write letters to the editor

It's the one way to appear in your local paper without having to pay, or be the focus of a feature. Handled properly, regular contributions to the "Letters to the editor" section are a great way to ensure that your name has a ring of familiarity about it when people are looking for a music teacher, while also communicating that you are a positive and creative force.

> **It's not just your name that they're learning.**
>
> **Readers will be able to tell from your writing that you're a highly interested expert who is prepared to go out of your way to praise good young musicians.**

I say "handled properly", because you're not free to use the forum to get just anything off your chest. Your students will be drawn from a wide range of backgrounds and political beliefs, and you don't want to risk alienating a large slice of them by putting forward the limerick you just penned about flag burning.

Instead of tackling political and moral conundrums, become a powerful positive force for the area you know best—music.

"At a time when teenagers seem to get nothing but bad press, I wanted to take a moment to give some praise. At the recent state instrumental championships, this town produced no fewer than 5 finalists in the under 16 category, while another fifty actually entered. Fifty! Instead of reserving column inches for car thefts and drug convictions, the names of these finalists should

```
have been displayed—how about some
good news for a change? To all who
took part, bravo!"
```

If your letter is a complaint, make sure it's something that people can be sympathetic to:

```
To the idiot who spoiled the final movement of
Mahler's 5th symphony the other night—leave your
cell phone at home next time! For it to ring was
one thing, but to actually ANSWER it...! Many of
this paper's readers would have been there, and
would have been as astonished as I was.
   Whoever you are, I hope you're reading this
and turning crimson. Great concert otherwise, for
those who missed it!
```

Be careful with this Golden Goose

You don't want to write in every week, otherwise the paper will grow weary of your musings almost as rapidly as the public does. But every few months it's worth putting *something* together and sending it in.

The aim is not for readers to suddenly want music lessons . It's so that by the time they *are* thinking about it, they've seen your name half a dozen times already — even if they can't quite put a finger on where.

But it's not just your *name* that they're learning. Readers will be able to tell from your writing that you are a highly interested expert who is prepared to go out of your way to praise good young musicians. Not everybody takes the time to write a letter to the editor, and the fact that you did — and that it was about music — will have been noted.

The end result? If you ask a random sample of newspaper readers to name someone who is a champion of music in town, your name will leap to mind.

Host your own radio show

Don't dismiss the idea just yet. It sounds preposterous at first, but it's not actually as far out of reach as you might think.

Most towns have community radio stations of some sort, staffed by volunteers. Most of these stations will be more than happy to talk to you about the possibility of a new show, particularly if you come to them with a well prepared outline of what's possible. Their station can only survive if people from the community take initiative and want to become involved, so it's not just you that your idea would be helping.

> **"But I could never host a show like that" I hear the protests saying.**
>
> **Nonsense. Music teachers already make their living talking.**

"But I could never host a show like that" I hear the protests saying. Nonsense. Music teachers already make their living talking. And because your area of expertise would be music, you'd probably spend 90% of the show simply playing music in any case.

In other words, a regular show does not have to mean dozens of hours of preparation and rehearsal. Let the music do most of the talking — you'd simply be introducing items, which is something you've done countless times before at student concerts.

So what would the show be about?

It's up to you, but I've included some ideas below, together with what would be required in order to make each idea a reality:

Composer of the week

You'd turn up armed with biography material, anecdotes, program notes and a pile of CDs to play, and listeners would end the show knowing a little more about Prokofieff than they used to.

Include some trivia about the composer, and some pieces that listeners probably haven't heard before.

This is a simple format, with a high ratio of music to talk, meaning that you don't have to work too hard once you're there.

Talent showcase

Another possibility is to dedicate the time to showcasing young promising students—they would come in and perform, and you would chat with them afterwards. This would be an enormous thrill for them (it will be probably be the first time they have appeared on radio), and you can bet that the whole family will be listening.

Don't just limit this to the instrument you teach though. Put the word out to *all* instrumental teachers that the opportunity exists, and let them nominate students who they feel are worthy. You should also contact local music competitions, and offer to automatically interview their finalists or winners.

As a community radio station, performers will know that the audience is not huge. (In fact, it probably is *only* their family!). That's not the point. The experience of playing on radio will be something they'll never forget, and is a welcome complement to the traditional recitals and competitions.

Mystery Composer

It's a popular format even within commercial music stations. The idea is that you dig up obscure works by a well known composer, together with obscure biographical details. As the show progresses, the clues will gradually become more helpful, until all is finally revealed at the end.

A little more research intensive than some other ideas, but a highly involving format for the listener (a lot of people can't stand not knowing, and will stay with you until the envelope is opened)

On this date...

There's no shortage of historical information available about music and musicians. If the show was airing on May 7th , then you might feature music by Brahms and Tchaikovsky (it's their birthday), and a movement from Beethoven's 9th (first performed on May 7 in 1824).

You might also mention that The Rolling Stones released the album "Exile on Main Street" on that date in 1972, and play "Tumbling Dice" and "Happy", which were the hit singles from that album.

There's no shortage of information like this available on the internet. The hard part is tracking down the recordings, but a local record store might agree to lend them to you in exchange for a mention on-air.

If you are running a show like this, make sure you let other music studios in town know about it.

It would be a novel way for their students to brush up on theory skills.

(It would also enable them to display a "Proud Sponsor of 2KMY Community Radio station" notice in store, without having to spend a cent)

On air Music theory and trivia quiz

Would obviously be for a niche audience only, but community radio stations are made with niche audiences in mind. The idea is that you'd fill the show with theory brainteasers and puzzles, and maybe play some music while they figure out the answers.

If you are running a show like this, make sure you let other music studios in town know about it. It would be a novel way for their students to brush up on theory skills.

You can lighten up the whole thing with some pointless music trivia — there's plenty to be found.

• Which famous composer wished to be buried

in white with six white horses pulling his hearse?

• Which Scandinavian composer had to be dragged out of the inn, usually by his wife, and forced to compose ?

• What pianist died during a performance of the Grieg Piano Concerto at Carnegie Hall in 1951?

Give some further clues for the answers, or again, play music while listeners think about the question (unlike a lesson, you can't simply sit in silence while your listener thinks about the answer)

Better still, if you want to create a genuine quiz atmosphere, have a panel that comes into the studio to answer the questions. The panel might be a team of students representing a particular music studio, as part of an ongoing theory quiz where different studios pit their expertise against each other. You ask the questions, they discuss the answer amongst themselves, and then lock it in. Trophies for the winner, and all good fun.

Oh — and in case you were wondering, the answers to those questions:

1. Eric Satie (no surprises there)

2. Jean Sibelius

3. Simon Barere (although I'm not sure if he was actually playing it at the time, or simply in the audience)

Again, if you're looking for an inexhaustible supply of music trivia, the internet is your best bet. Music theory brainteasers you would probably have to create yourself, but you'll have no problem coming up with some tough ones if you need to.

This week in the arts

There are usually plenty of concerts, plays and exhibitions going on in town, and it might be worthwhile dedicating a show to highlighting what's coming up. On commercial radio, it's going to be difficult for such events to get more than a thirty

185

second advertisement, or a few minutes for an interview, but on community radio there are rarely such time pressures.

Most people are very keen to promote their own performances if possible, so it should be possible to organize plenty of interviews with the key organizers and players — creating a powerful vehicle for you to network with other musicians and artists in town.

> **If parents tune in to hear their own child take part in your "Trivia Quiz", and hear participants having plenty of fun...**
>
> **...they'll assume that your lessons are likely to be plenty of fun too.**

A mixed bag

Your show could actually be a combination of the ideas above, with the whole format divided into segments. So it starts with "Composer of the week", then features a talented young student, followed by a trivia quiz and then "This Week in the arts" to finish.

Make sure though that you are clear on both the proposed format, and the resources you would need before you approach the station itself. They're much more likely to be interested if they can actually picture the show for themselves, can see that the groundwork has been done already, and can see evidence that the format is sustainable.

The benefits of your own show

While it's certainly not impossible, having your own regular radio show will involve plenty of careful work. So how does it help?

Name recognition

Community radio is never going to have an enormous audience, but very fact that the show exists will help promote the name of your studio—particularly if your show involves other students. When they perform on-air for the first time in their lives, you can bet their family and friends will be tuned in. The performer might not even play the instrument you teach—but their little sister might.

Similarly, if parents tune in to hear their own child take part in your "Trivia Quiz", and hear participants having plenty of fun, they'll assume that your lessons are likely to be plenty of fun too.

Refer to it in your other advertising

How many teachers do you know who have their own radio show? Once it becomes known that you do, it will be hard not to picture you having plenty of drive and initiative, and being an interesting person. If you want your studio to stand out from the crowd, then having something unusual like a radio show on your CV doesn't hurt. So once your show is up and running, don't be shy about it—refer to it whenever you have the space.

> **How many teachers do you know who have their own radio show?**
>
> **Once it becomes known that you do, it will be hard not to picture you having plenty of drive and initiative, and being an interesting person.**

Benefits continue even after the show stops

Your show may well end at some stage, but nobody can ever take away from you the fact that it once existed. You can add "Radio broadcaster" to your CV permanently, helping you reap benefits from your adventure long after the final show goes to air.

Use it to promote your own studio and students

It's your show. If you have a student who has just won a competition, or you have a studio recital to promote, or are offering a scholarship and calling for auditions, you can use your show as a promotion vehicle. You have to be careful that the entire show doesn't start to sound like an advertisement for your studio, but there's nothing wrong with giving your students an occasional plug.

Become well known to colleagues

Your show has the potential to offer a huge range of exciting opportunities for other teachers—they can showcase their best students, they can promote upcoming concerts, or come in and chat with you about their area of expertise. All of these things help them promote their own studio.

To make these things happen, all they need to do is contact you. It's a great way not only to become known to a wide community of music teachers, but to be a focal point for the entire community.

The hardest thing about your own radio show...

Is getting up the courage to approach a radio station in the first place. It's not like you have a background in radio—but then again, neither did any of their presenters when they first began.

Exciting opportunities await the music teachers who have the courage to be the person in town who actually does this.

You want to make sure it's you, and not someone else.

Public Bulletin Boards

Not all studio promotion techniques have to be sophisticated or expensive. Just about every shopping center features public bulletin boards—a place where people can post notices about jobs wanted, lost pets, missing people, or advertisements for their own small businesses.

The vast majority of people who pass by will ignore the board—but with such a large volume of traffic every day, even if only one person in a thousand takes a moment to stop and read, your message will have been seen by a *lot* of people before the year is out.

Ensure that your poster presents professionally, and has tear off strips at the bottom with your phone number and

> **Even if just *one* student calls because of the poster, that suddenly makes the bulletin board worth hundreds of dollars to you - thousands over a period of several years.**

website address. The tabs aren't just there so that people can take your phone number—they also provide a quick way for you to tell whether or not your notice is actually being noticed.

It can all feel like a depressing filter—not everyone who passes by will stop, not everyone who stops will read your ad, not everyone who reads your ad will take the phone number, and not everyone who takes the number will call.

But you're not placing this poster hoping to attract twenty new students. Even if just one student calls because of the poster, that suddenly makes the bulletin board worth hundreds of dollars to you—thousands over a period of several years.

How to find the bulletin boards

They're everywhere, but can take a little finding in the first place. All you really need to do is keep your eyes open when you next go shopping, and have your notebook handy. Record the locations of the boards as you discover them, together with impressions you have about how heavy the pedestrian traffic is likely to be for the area. You also need to ensure that parents of potential students are well represented among the passers-by — ten thousand daily visitors are no use to you if the bulletin board is in an army mess hall.

There are plenty of places that act as magnets for families, and many of them have bulletin boards:

- Child care centers
- Supermarkets
- School reception areas
- Medical Center waiting areas
- Indoor adventure playground centers
- Fast food outlets
- Public Libraries
- Food courts

You also need to check the bulletin boards for any notices about the correct procedure for posting a notice. If you're supposed to ask for permission, then ask for permission.

Once you have a list of half a dozen boards, print your posters and put them up.

Maintaining your ad

Once you've put the poster up, you'll need to check back regularly to make sure that you don't need to replace it. Posters are subject to being moved or removed, can be obscured partially or completely by newer posters, and may end up covered in graffiti, or in close proximity to unsuitable posters. (You don't really want your poster being partially covered by a notice about "Exotic Dancers at Club Jiggles")

When any of these things happen, simply put up a fresh poster. If you find that this means a new poster every few days, then unless your phone is already ringing, you need to find a new bulletin board.

The other reason you may need to replace the poster is if all the tear-off phone numbers have been taken. Your poster is not much good to you if readers cannot contact you.

If this all feels like too much work, or it's not going to be possible for you to visit the bulletin board regularly to assess them for maintenance, then this is the wrong strategy for you. An obscured poster is no use to you at all, while a graffitied poster might actually end up being harmful for the image of your studio. Bulletin boards are potentially useful because they are free and accessible—but those are the very qualities that can leave them open to abuse.

Helping your poster stand out

Having your poster physically obscured is not the only threat to it not being seen. It can be front and center on the bulletin board, and still rendered all but invisible if it too closely resembles the posters around it.

So how do you ensure that it stands out from the crowd?

Unfortunately, you can't always answer that in advance. If you really want to be certain of standing out, you have to assess what's already there. If most of the posters are printed on yellow paper, make sure yours is a light red. If most of the posters use center aligned text on standard copy paper, then make yours right aligned on half-letter.

There are also some unconventional posters you can use that will contrast with just about anything. Most posters are rectangular, so make yours a circle. Or use scissors to give it a jagged edge. Or fold cardboard to create a 3D ad that literally jumps off the board.

Or in an age of computer printouts, make yours the only one that uses genuine calligraphy. Or the only ad that leaves most of the page blank, instead of trying to pack it with information. Or the only one that is designed to look and feel like a personal letter.

As long as the tone of the poster is still consistent with assumptions you want people to make about your studio, design is up to you, and the more creative you can be, the more likely people are to stop and read it in the first place. More than that, a highly creative poster will suggest that your teaching is likely to be creative too—not a bad first introduction for parents who might otherwise know nothing about you yet.

Involve yourself in the community

Most students live within a short drive of their teacher's studio—if they didn't, they'd probably be having lessons with someone else. There are plenty of other music teachers in the Yellow Pages, and one of the first things parents look for is proximity.

This means that your potential students probably share the same zip code you do. They shop in the same malls, they eat at the same restaurants. They send their kids to the same schools, order pizza from the same take-aways, and have picnics in the same parks.

> **If you want your local community to respond favorably to you—or even to know you *exist*— it's time to get involved.**

When it's raining on your house, they're getting wet too.

All of this means that your local community is not just the people that you live near. It's also the wellspring that feeds your studio.

If you want that community to respond favorably to you—or even to know you exist—it's time to get involved.

Get involved how?

The options are endless, so you have no excuse for not being able to find something that interests you. Coach a junior soccer team. Volunteer to read stories to kids at the local library. Go doorknocking for charities. Take part in tree planting programs.

Become active in community based committees—neighborhood watch, PTA, choral society, local theater...anything that needs meetings and people to contribute.

Instead of just reading about the annual "Clean up our town" day, roll up your sleeves and get involved. Turn up for fun runs— even if you're not actually participating, you can still supervise a drinks station.

Your mantra needs to be "Hi—I'm here to help. I'm a music teacher, so I've got plenty of experience in working with kids. Just let me know what I can do."

So how does this help?

Apart from making your life richer and more interesting, becoming involved in your local community will put you in countless positions where you can talk to people that you might never have met otherwise.

And part of these conversations will be the inevitable question:

> *"So, tell me — what do you do for a living?"*

Not only is the fact that you're music teacher memorable because it's a little unusual, it's an occupation that lends itself easily to follow-up conversation.

> **You don't need to advertise yourself, or push in any way. Just answer the question "So tell me—what do you do for a living" when it comes up.**

Often simply finding out that you're a music teacher can be an ice-breaker, prompting choruses of "Really? I had lessons as a child once, and my mother used to play the violin" — it's amazing how people take it as a cue to open up a little. (If you don't believe me, compare the reaction you get if you explain that you're a bank clerk, or in insurance sales instead.)

The end result? Your community involvement will mean that you are introduced to hundreds of people you never might have met otherwise. Some of these people will have kids looking for lessons — in fact some of these people will *be* kids looking for lessons.

You don't need to advertise yourself, or push in any way. Just answer the question "So tell me—what do you do for a living" when it comes up.

Volunteer to be the media liaison for the event

"In the studio this morning we have Michael Langmack, who will be one of thousands of volunteers rolling up their sleeves to help with Sunday's "Make Midville Beautiful" cleanup...Michael, welcome to the program."

During the course of the interview it will be revealed that Michael is a local music teacher. How? Because he was answering a question on the astonishing *breadth* of participants, and simply used what he did for a living as an example. And if he wants the fact that he is a music teacher to get more air time still? All he has to do is throw it in to some of his other answers.

"That's a good question, but here's the thing — musicians have a reputation for not wanting to get dirty hands...I'm here to tell you that if I can do this, anyone can. Come down to the old Boatshed on Sunday at 10 am, and we'll give you a cleanup kit. I've got twenty-five of my own students turning up."

Obviously you don't use the opportunity to actually *advertise* your studio in any way. All you do is mention what you do for a living. And in the minds of thousands of parents who are listening, because of your enthusiasm, your obvious contributions to the community, and your self-confidence on radio, you've earned a small tick.

Sometimes a small tick is all it takes.

MASTERCLASS: **Stop thinking like a musician**

It should be one of our greatest assets, but for many music teachers, it proves to be a fatal flaw:

The fact that most music teachers were once highly capable music students themselves.

We've been to masterclasses and workshops, we've performed difficult pieces, won trophies and praise in competitions, and stood out from our peers at school as being "musically talented". More than that, we've had a fuss made over us by family and friends, all proud of our aptitude and skills.

Many of us are from musical families, were exposed to music at a young age, and have had mentors and significant adults who have been musicians in their own right. And if we have undertaken tertiary studies in music at some stage, then there would have been a large slice of our lives where most of our waking hours were dedicated to music.

> **When you construct your ads, you have to look at them through the eyes of parents, *not* the eyes of another musician.**

We have. But most of our students haven't, and never will.

Incubated in a world dominated by music, it can be hard for us to remember this—*but if you forget it, you risk alienating the people you are trying to attract.*

Reflect what they're looking for

When you construct your ads, you have to look at them through the eyes of parents, *not* the eyes of another musician. No matter how proud you might be of your University Medal winning Masters thesis on Flemish Polyphony, it's not something you should mention in your advertisement. But the fact that parents are welcome to sit in on lessons *is* something to highlight. Similarly, you may well have been a finalist in a National Concerto competition when only a teenager. But for your ads, that's nothing beside the fact that you provide special help sessions for parents who want to support their kids while they practice.

The tempting thing when writing an ad is to start listing your CV. Before including any item though, you have to ask the question that parents will ask anyway:

How will that help a child learn to play?

If the answer is not immediately clear, then the item is using up valuable advertising space that would be better allocated demonstrating a genuine benefit of working with you.

Hear what they're really saying.

A great way to fine tune your instincts for what parents are *really* looking for is to listen carefully during interviews, and actually ask them the question "So what are you hoping for from these music lessons?". Their answer might not be the one that you would have given, but it's the answer that counts.

The phrases that keep coming up in such conversations would then become the phrases that your advertising should actually include—that way you can intelligently *anticipate* what your potential students will be checking the ad for, rather than simply listing a bunch of features and then hoping.

It's the reason that most businesses will use focus groups before deciding how to pitch their new products. No matter how proud Ford might be that their new car has poly-traction computer assisted four wheel braking, if the focus group was overwhelmingly more excited about the fact that the back seat has it's own separate DVD player, then that's what will feature in the ad. It will break the engineers' hearts, but it will sell a lot more cars.

Mentoring for new teachers

This is a powerful but subtle promotion tool, although it's really only possible to pursue with any credibility if you have been teaching for a decade or more already.

The logic is that you would provide a free **mentoring service** for new music teachers who are trying to establish themselves — your role is to help them find their way as they take their first tentative steps into what should end up being a rewarding career. You can then use the very existence of the scheme to help promote your own studio.

The experience edge

Your years of teaching mean that you will have insights that no university course can impart — everything from studio policies, to dealing with difficult

> **You can use the very existence of the scheme to help promote your own studio**

parents, to running studio recitals. New teachers will figure all this out given time — your mentoring program is there to make sure they don't have to, fast tracking them to a successful studio of their own.

How can this possibly help your teaching studio?

This strategy is a good example of the power of *indirect promotion*. For this mentoring scheme to work, it will need to be something that you announce — probably with a small newspaper advertisement:

NOTICE TO NEW MUSIC TEACHERS

Jane Hemphill of **Hemphill Oboe Studios** will be interviewing new teachers to take part in her **teacher mentoring** program. Participation is free—the aim being to help new teachers orientate themselves in this rewarding career by providing support and advice through the critical first few months.

Jane Hemphill is one of Midville's best known music teachers, with over **18 years experience** teaching oboe to students of all ages. Interested teachers should call **855-4498-0091** to organize an interview.

The real value of this ad is not that new teachers will see it—although many will. It's that plenty of *parents of prospective students will see it too.*

The assumption will be that if you are running a mentoring program for other teachers, that you must be a Master Teacher of some sort. (If you've been teaching for 18 years, that's probably not far off the mark!)

It all helps lend an air of credibility and expertise to your studio—the logic being that a teacher to other teachers must be a fine teacher indeed.

You need to be confident in your own background and experience before considering this, but it's a useful option for teachers who already have plenty of runs on the board.

The benefits of an ongoing association

The teachers you helped will also remember that you took the time to get them started. If in the future they are either full, or have a student who has outgrown them, you're almost certainly going to be the person they recommend for further study. After all, you were the person who helped train them, something that would come as high recommendation indeed for the parents involved.

To help maintain the relationship once the initial mentoring period is over, offer to hear their students every semester as part of the mentoring service. You would run a workshop, and then spend an hour or so afterwards chatting with the teacher about your impressions. Quite apart from being a valuable way for your protege to debrief after an Event, the whole exercise will help keep your name prominent in the mind of that teacher, and the collective minds of the students and their families. Remember — although you wouldn't actively suggest such a thing — once these students become sufficiently advanced, they might just end up being *your* students.

> **It all helps lend an air of credibility and expertise to your studio...**
>
> **...the logic being that a teacher to other teachers must be a fine teacher indeed.**

This might not be such an exciting proposition if you just have an association with a single studio, but if you have mentored a *dozen* such teachers, the flow into your studio from such "graduating" students can be enough to keep your schedule full with no other promotion required.

Establish a support group

If you find yourself with several respondents to your advertisement, you should consider setting up a regular meeting for all the teachers involved. That way they can swap frustrations and war stories, while you moderate and throw in possible solutions to the problems they couldn't cope with.

You should also encourage former participants to take part in these meetings, helping establish a feeling of community among those teachers you've helped, and maintaining the relationships long after the need for help has gone.

Promotional Merchandise

No matter how well developed your desktop publishing skills, sometimes the most creative way to get your message across is to abandon the idea of paper entirely. Promotional merchandise allows you to create advertisements that people can wear, use and touch — providing a fun way of promoting your studio that transcends the traditional boundaries of print-based advertising.

> **Sometimes the most creative way to get your message across is to abandon the idea of paper entirely.**

So instead of simply having your message appearing on a poster or brochure, it can appear on a baseball cap. Or a clock. Or a pen. The idea is to turn your advertisement into a *gift*.

Digital printing processes now make it possible to print on just about anything you like, giving you options for promotional merchandise that will be both fun, attention-getting and limited only by your imagination. Given that they are designed to advertise your studio, you shouldn't charge for them — put the production costs down as an advertising expense, and then give the items away to your students. You'll think of plenty of your own ideas, but some possibilities are below to get you started:

- **Mousepads.** Make sure it features the name of your studio website prominently (see p 223), and then have the mousepads as giveaways on the front counter at your local music store. as part of a reciprocated advertising arrangement. Even if customers don't end up *taking* the mousepad, it's a novel way of having them absorb the fact that you have a website, giving them yet another reason for them to check it out.

- **T-Shirts/baseball caps** A great medium, because it offers plenty of space for both a fun picture and big message. In fact, the more fun you can make it to look at, the more likely kids are to wear it to the shops, at school camp...wherever. In short, if you create a great T-shirt or cap, you can turn your students into your own willing and walking billboards

• **Pencils/pens.** Easily portable, cheap to get printed and likely to end up being used at school. If you really want to make it useful for your students, get your studio's name printed on a set of coloring pencils or markers. With the way students end up lending pens to each other, your message is not just likely to be seen by other students, but will often end up in other households.

• **Fridge Magnets.** Great for your students, but even better as an alternative to a conventional mailout campaign. Instead of putting two hundred brochures in letterboxes, put two hundred fridge magnets instead.

• **Bags.** For library books, sports clothes — whatever. Again, make sure the design would be neutral enough to be genuinely useful for activities outside music lessons, but that the name of your studio is prominent nonetheless.

Digital printing processes now make it possible to print on just about anything you like...

... giving you options for promotional merchandise that will be both fun, attention-getting and limited only by your imagination.

• **Photo frame.** Don't just supply the empty frame — include a photo of the child in action at their recent concert, so that it's the sort of thing that might end up on mum's desk at work.

• **Wine opener.** An end-of-year gift for the parents in your studio. It then ends up advertising your studio as it sits on the table at gatherings of family and friends. Again, it's an unusual promotion item, and is likely to start conversations. (If for no other reason than people will be wondering why on earth a wine opener has the name of a music school on it!)

• **Post-it notepads.** Inexpensive to produce, and sooner or later the household will find uses for it. Your logo should not be too prominent - maybe a watermark, or small tag in the bottom right corner.

• **Calendar.** It's a favorite with businesses as a promotional item, largely because every family needs one, and once there, it's referred to regularly for a whole year. Personalize with photos of the student at their lessons, and messages about practicing.

• **Metronome.** It's the essential tool of the practicing trade, so it might as well have the name of your studio on it. This is an item that you might be able to sell to students—the idea being that you could purchase and print on them in bulk, and then pass on the savings to your students. Again, it's the sort of item your local music store might agree to display instead of a poster as part of a reciprocal advertising arrangement. (Would look very cool—and appropriate— on the front counter.)

• **Watches.** Your studio's name would be printed either on the band, or on the face behind the numbers if it's an analogue watch, and you've got yourself another readily portable advertisement.

• **Studio CD.** If you have your own recording facilities, you can produce CDs of each your students playing. Proud parents then often request multiple copies to give to family and friends as presents (I once had a student request 35 copies of their son's CD!). This becomes a promotion tool on many levels, but above all has people marvelling that such a thing is even possible in the first place—and then wondering what else might be possible in your studio.

How to get these items custom printed

Your local copy shop should have the technology to take care of a lot of these items, while a quick search for Promotional Merchandise in the Yellow Pages will give you the contact details of companies that can cope with the tougher items.

There are usually significant savings for getting things printed in bulk, so it might be worth creating enough units for several years of giveaways. Like many effective promotion ideas, you need to be ready to spend money to get a good result.

There are also plenty of companies online that can help—do a Google Search for "Promotional Merchandise" to find businesses that can cater to your area. You simply upload or email your graphics file, choose the item you want to be personalized, and enter your address and credit card details. The items will then be printed, and delivered to your studio door.

> **There are usually significant savings for getting things printed in bulk, so it might be worth creating enough units for several years of giveaways.**

Using the stores for inspiration

The ideas outlined in this chapter are by no means comprehensive. The range of objects that can be printed on is growing all the time—a great way to get new ideas is to actually browse a print store with an open mind, whether it's the local Kwik Kopy house, or an online solution. Chat to the staff, tell them about your business, and ask them for recommendations. If the items they show you strike you as being fun and useful, then they'll probably strike your students the same way.

At the end of the day, your advertisement will feel to students like a *present*, so it's not only a means of promoting your studio...it's also a novel way of rewarding students you already work with.

Write your own *column*

Not all of the columns you read in newspapers are contributed by in-house staff. Some of them are reprints of articles that appear in other papers, but plenty of others are contributed by free-lance writers. In other words, apart from the column itself, there is no relationship between the paper and the journalist.

> **If you're handy with a word-processor, it might be time to put together a series of articles, and launch your own column.**

These free-lance writers are often not writers by profession—they are simply experts in their particular fields, which then becomes the focus of their column. So the long time owner of the largest rods and tackle store in town might create a column on great spots for fishing. A doctor might create a column on recognizing and coping with common family ailments.

These writers will sometimes forgo payment of any kind, in return for a byline that mentions where they work.

Well, guess what. You're an expert too. And the area that you are an expert in is of interest to plenty of readers. If you're handy with a word-processor, it might be time to put together a series of articles, and launch your own column.

Suggestions for content

When creating the blueprint for your own column, you have to think in terms of what's likely to be useful and interesting for readers, rather than simply writing about what you know most about. So you may well know plenty about 17th Century tuning systems, but that's not the sort of thing people want to read about while they eat their toast. However, a series of light articles on the lives and scandals of famous composers just might be—particularly if you can tie that in to concerts that are happening in town.

So what can you write about? It's up to you, but some

possibilities include:

Profiles of local musicians

As a musician yourself, you'll know the right questions to ask. The idea is that you would interview a different musician each time — some up and coming, others already established. It all helps the paper create the impression of a thriving arts scene in town, which in turn will make the section an attractive proposition for advertisers in the field. So underneath your fortnightly column about a local music star might be ads for shows, or music instrument stores, or even other teachers advertising their studios.

Previews of upcoming concerts in town

Program details, rumors, cancellations, information about visiting soloists, dates, venues — everything anybody in town with an interest in music would need to keep their calendar full and the box offices buzzing.

It might also be possible for you to interview some of these visiting artists, helping you build a reputation by association. (It might not be too, but you should definitely try)

> **...you need to be armed with some statistics that demonstrate just how many families in town are involved with music lessons.**
>
> **Fortunately, that figure is always an attrative one.**

Advice for young musicians

Before an editor would agree to a column with subject matter as specific as this, you'd need to be armed with some information about just how many families in town are involved with music lessons. Fortunately, that figure is always an attractive one.

Your column would be then be there to provide support and advice on everything from pre-concert nerves, to how parents can help their child practice.

Previews of upcoming *school* concerts

Everything from end of year plays, to musicals, to talent nights, to organized recitals. If one of the local infant's schools is putting on a production of Fairy Tales, people will hear about it first in your column, and you can give some of the "stars" a thrill by actually mentioning their name in the column. The idea is that your column becomes a place through which schools can announce their upcoming musical adventures, helping ensure that the production itself gets the audience it deserves.

Your column would then not just be of interest to those who are actually in the productions. Students will be able to read about their school, even if they are not personally in the performance itself. As far as the paper is concerned, you would be giving several communities each week a new reason to want to by a copy of the paper — and some of these communities will consist of many hundreds of families.

It also ensures that your name is known to all the schools involved, which can be enormously useful for any other future relationship you may want to develop with that school.

Who to approach

• Smaller local papers are the best bet — not only are they more likely to say yes to the offer of a column (particularly if you are prepared to do it for free), their readership also overlaps neatly with the area from which your students are typically drawn.

• Family based magazines, usually with plenty of material on parenting and education. The magazine probably won't have a section on music lessons yet — your job is to have them hitting themselves on the forehead as they wonder why they didn't think of it before. Again, make sure you're armed with figures about how many families have kids taking music lessons.

• School newsletters. Your "column" might be as simple as "Practice Tip of the month", but with hundreds of children in most schools learning musical instruments, it will be useful advice. School newsletters are also a great way of profiling a "Musical Star of the Month" — one of the students who might have a concert coming up, or who performed well in a recent competition, or maybe just someone who has made rapid and remarkable progress in their first three months of lessons. Let other music teachers know that they are welcome to nominate deserving students for this category.

> **The rewards for just one publication saying yes are worth the pain of collecting dozens of rejection letters.**

Rotation policy on rejections

There is no guarantee that the editor will be interested in your proposed column, and you may well end up receiving a polite "thanks but no thanks" note in response. If that happens, don't give up — simply target a different publication. The rewards for just one publication saying yes are worth the pain of collecting dozens of rejection letters.

And if they all say no? Move on. It's not like you're short on promotion ideas now.

You can always rework your material and try again next year.

Start a choir or ensemble

This is a simple idea that provides a rich variety of promotion opportunities for your studio. The plan is to set up your own choir or ensemble, hold weekly rehearsals, and then organize performances. You'd become the conductor, ensemble manager, motivator and coach for the ensemble members, and would be creating an opportunity for dozens of young musicians that might not be available to them otherwise.

> **One of the most reliable sources of new students is families that are already participating in music lessons of some sort.**

We'll take a look in a moment at how to set the whole thing up, but how does running such an ensemble help you promote your own studio?

Targeting the families who are most likely to come aboard.

One of the most reliable sources of new students is families that are already participating in music lessons of some sort.

This is partly because such families don't need to be convinced that music lessons are worthwhile — they've already seen them in action, and have experienced the positive difference they can make.

But it's mostly because of the powerful influence of sibling role models. Craig's sister learns the clarinet. Craig's brother learns the violin. As soon as Craig is old enough, it will often feel like a natural progression for him to have music lessons of his own too. In fact, if he is not at least presented with the opportunity, he'll probably feel left out.

You want to ensure that you are on Craig's parents' short list for possible music teachers — which means that his family has to know who you are, even if none of their kids currently learns the instrument you teach.

The beauty of setting up your own ensemble is that you don't need to find such families. Instead, they find you, because your new ensemble is really a collection of students *who are already having music lessons.* And in the process you'll meet their families, and will be on the short list straight away when the younger siblings are looking for lessons.

The power of performances

Some of the best ads for your studio are really in disguise. No matter how strong the relationship with your local school, they're highly unlikely to allow you to spend half an hour promoting your studio to students and parents. But they would normally jump at the chance of your ensemble giving a free concert for half an hour.

That thirty minutes of music will be a better advocate for your studio than any Powerpoint presentation from you ever could have been. The enthusiasm, focus and musicianship of your ensemble will speak for itself.

Being seen as a mover and shaker

Ensembles don't just happen. Your concerts won't only speak volumes about your creativity and musicianship — they'll also be a tribute to your ability to organize and motivate yourself and others, and you'll perceived as a teacher with initiative.

Well, guess what. If you go ahead and set up an ensemble like this, you *are* teacher with initiative, and you'll deserve every reward that comes your way.

Why will students want to be involved?

The success of this idea is predicated upon securing participants, but that's not as difficult as you might imagine. Aside from bands at school, learning an instrument can be a lonely experience. Your ensemble will give students a rare chance to work with other musicians, and to experience the magic of the whole being greater than the sum of its parts.

And if your focus happens to be chamber music, your ensemble might be the *only* opportunity they have for music making with a small group.

In short, it helps answer the question "So I know how to play a musical instrument—how am I going to have *fun* now that I can?"

Their own teachers will also not be blind to the impact participation can have on their sight reading, ensemble skills and sense of musicianship, and many will be keenly encouraging participation to their own students.

And the clincher? Offer pizza at the end of rehearsals.☺

Getting started

The first thing you'll need is access to a **rehearsal space.** Your local school may be willing to help with this, particularly if you make it clear that the ensemble is directed towards students from the school, and that you will agree to perform at assemblies or other special functions as requested. You might even offer to feature the name of the school in the ensemble's title, so that the whole exercise becomes an ambassador for the school itself.

> In short, it helps answer the question "So I know how to play a musical instrument...how am I going to have *fun* now that I can?"

Failing that, you might be able to convert a garage or living room at home. You don't have to accommodate rehearsals for Mahler 8, and if space is genuinely an issue, then keep the ensembles small. It might be a quartet rather than an octet, or small *a capella* choir.

You then need to find **repertoire**. There are special libraries that will lend music for purposes like this—the best way to start is to actually talk to conductors of existing ensembles. They'll be able to help you find what you need, and give you a better understanding of any paperwork or costs involved. If you're not experienced as an ensemble conductor, they might also be able to give you some tips as to what sort of repertoire might be appropriate, together with details of traps to avoid.

Armed with a space to rehearse in, and repertoire to rehearse with, you then need to **get the word out** that the opportunity exists. Put together a letter to send to other music teachers, with details on what the ensemble is trying to achieve, together with what specific benefits it is aiming to bring for participants.

But probably the best way to fish for participants is to make an announcement at a local school assembly. Reinforce this by posting some fliers in the music rooms at the school, together with ensuring that the front office has all the information they need to handle any enquiries:

STRING AND WOODWIND PLAYERS WANTED

If you sound good by yourself, you won't believe how good you'll sound with other musicians of your age. **Harmony Players** is a brand new group directed by Heather Simpson from the Simpson Clarinet Studio—there'll be plenty of **concerts, fun** rehearsals, and then **pizza** at the end of every get together.

Forms available from your music teacher.

Work with what you get

Don't expect your ensemble to attract dozens of students straight away. It can take time to grow, meaning that when you first start, numbers might be low, and the instruments could well be oddly balanced.

So if your call for "Young musicians of all types" means that you end up with two tubas, a harp, bagpipes and a heavy metal guitarist, don't panic—think creatively. The very fact that the ensemble is so strange can make it interesting to audiences even before a single note is played. If the task feels beyond you, issue a challenge to the composition department of your local tertiary music school—give them a style, the ensemble details and the fact that you'll give the composer concerned a big plug at the concert. (If they can make the ensemble above work, then they *deserve* a big plug!)

Don't discount students from your own studio as possible group members — obviously their participation won't be introducing you to families that you don't already know, but they will help flesh out the ensemble, giving it the appearance of being bustling and successful.

Give regular concerts

Your single best recruiting tool for the ensemble is to give performances, so you want them to be frequent and as high profile as possible. At the end of each performance, put out the call to the audience — let them know that the group is always looking out for new members, and that all they need to do is present themselves at one of your rehearsals. Be friendly, be welcoming, and be clear on what's involved. Then give them the rest of your performance itinerary so that they can see what's waiting for them at the end of all the hard work.

How are you going to fill an itinerary like that? Start with schools — tell them that it will be a free performance, by young musicians, for young musicians. Your aim is for students in the audience to go home practicing a little harder, and then wondering how they can be involved in your group.

Other ideas for groups

Your ensembles don't just have to be about performance. Other ideas to consider:

• A **composition group**, where members would write works for the ensemble, and then help perform works by other group members.

• Regular **improvisation workshop**. Outside of jazz, improvisation is a dying art, but students who master it can elegantly and credibly get themselves out of trouble on stage.

• **Theory group**. Students solve problems together, and set problems for other students. Co-operative learning, and an alternative to the dry approach of fill-in-the-book.

• Provide **background music for a theatrical production**. Your ensemble would create, rehearse and perform the music for the play.

Create a feeling of belonging

If you want students to be excited about your new group, you have to make it larger than life. It should have its own newsletter, filled with profiles of group members, details of upcoming rehearsals and concerts, profiles of upcoming repertoire and the featured composers, together with music trivia, jokes and photos of the group and group members.

You should also consider creating an ensemble **uniform**. It doesn't have to be anything fancy — just a logo laser printed on to a T-shirt will be fine, perhaps with a matching cap. The idea is to make participants feel welcome, and for it to be tough to want to leave.

Involve the members of the group in every aspect of the ensemble's management, from repertoire preferences, to seating arrangements, to the design and distribution of posters advertising performances, to the way the ensemble takes its bows. That way the performances they create are truly their own, and they can feel ownership and pride in the behind the scenes work, as well as the delivery of the music itself.

The aim is to have students leaving every rehearsal buzzing — it doesn't then take a huge leap of imagination on the part of parents to assume that your lessons must be well thought out and loads of fun too.

The end result is that one day, one of these parents will take you aside and mention to you that they have a younger child who has been considering private music lessons...do you have any spaces?

MASTERCLASS: Tracking your Results

Whatever promotion elements you end up adopting, simply planning and executing a promotion campaign is not enough. Once the dust has settled from the year that was, you need to review each aspect of the campaign, and assess it for the impact it had on your student numbers.

> It's been said of advertising that fifty cents in each dollar is wasted—the problem is knowing *which* fifty cents.
>
> Tracking your results can help you find out.

This means that you will need to implement some sort of tracking system. As every new enquiry comes in, one of your questions *has* to be "How did you hear about me?". If twelve months goes past and nobody mentions your carefully designed newspaper ads, then there's no point in flogging that particular dead horse.

On the other hand, if every third enquiry refers to your letterbox drop, then it might be worth investing in widening the area of the drop. Or considering a color brochure. Or a *second* drop half way through the year. Or creating a brand new "2 Free Lessons" promotion, but announcing it through a letterbox drop, rather than taking up space in your Yellow Pages ad.

It's been said of advertising that fifty cents in every dollar is wasted—the problem is knowing which fifty cents. Tracking your results can help you find out.

Keeping the records you need

The simplest way to take care of this is to keep a book by the phone, and record the details as soon as each enquiry comes in. Alternatively, if you have your own free PracticePage studio management website (see p 226), you can record the details in your "Enquiry Manager"—it will allow you to record exactly how the enquirer heard about your studio. Either way, don't even think about organizing next year's advertising until you understand how effective *this* year's was .

Don't get sentimental

Tracking is there to tell you the truth about your campaigns, not the things you'd like to hear. From time to time you'll be shocked to discover that your favorite element is not performing as it should. In fact, it might not be performing at all.

You can certainly try to tweak it a little—maybe you can write better copy, or be smarter about how you implement the idea. But if it doesn't respond to first aid like this, it's time to declare this horse dead, and move on to something else.

As this book demonstrates, there are plenty of other promotion ideas waiting to take its place.

Swap war stories

You're not the only teacher trying to promote their own studio, and wrestling with different promotion ideas. The next time your MTA has a meeting, put advertising campaigns on the agenda—the idea being for the teachers present to be able to compare their own experiences of particular promotion tactics. Armed with the triumphs and horror stories of their peers, everyone comes away better able to shape their own advertisements for the future.

In other words, if you discover a great promotion tactic, you don't necessarily have to guard it as though it's the location of a sunken wreck filled with treasure. If the teaching profession as a whole in your town starts promoting music lessons more effectively, it helps to drive up demand for music lessons in general.

Unleashing the power of the internet

Using a studio website to *attract* new students...

...and then to astound them at the interview

(We've built your website for you - all you have to do is move in)

Studio web advertisement

Your poster at the local shop has a potential audience of hundreds. Your newspaper ad, tens of thousands.

But if you want a direct link to the homes of every potential student in town, there's only one way to do it. You need a webpage. It will work for you 24 hours a day, 7 days a week, and provide a depth of information about your studio that your conventional advertising never could.

Not only that, you can update the information instantly, with no extra printing costs, or the need to recall existing materials.

> To set up your own free studio web advertisement instantly, simply go to the PracticeSpot Press website at:
> **www.practicespot.com**

How to set up your webpage

The PracticeSpot Press official website will allow you to set up your very own studio promotion webpage instantly, and for free — and best of all, you don't need to know anything about building webpages to do it. Just fill in the blanks. To see an example of a finished product , go to:

`www.janmurray.practicespot.com`

Or you can set up your own simply by going to:

`www.practicespot.com`

and create your own "My PracticeSpot" account. (It takes around 20 seconds, and it won't cost you a cent)

What your webpage will contain

Your PracticeSpot Webpage has been set up to display a huge range of information about your studio, but you can actually turn off any of the sections that don't seem relevant. You can also edit or update any of the sections at any time, allowing your ad to evolve as your studio does. So what will your ad contain? That's up to you, but the following sections are there ready to be filled in:

Where to find the studio

Allows you to display the address of your studio, together with any notes you want to include on how to find the studio—cross streets, landmarks, distinguishing characteristics of the studio itself.

If your studio is based in the United States, a map can automatically be displayed showing the location of your studio.

Contact details

Ensures that interested parents will have plenty of different ways of getting in touch with you, allowing you to display your phone number, cell phone, fax and email address.

About the teacher

Helps make your background three dimensional for visitors to your webpage. Provides sections in which you can detail:
- Your teaching history
- Qualifications
* Association Memberships
- Testimonials (You can either list them or indicate "available on request")
- Other interests—Hobbies etc.
- Student success stories
- Strengths (don't be modest)
- Weaknesses (and don't water it down)
- Any other relevant information

What the studio offers students

Your chance to outline exactly what it is that makes your studio unique, while also helping visitors judge for themselves whether your particular niche is relevant to their needs. Provides sections in which you can detail:

- Mission statement
- Principal Instrument taught
- Other instruments taught
- Principal style taught
- Other styles taught
- Studio size
- Studio specialties (e.g.. beginners, music technology)
- Whether you have instruments for hire
- Whether sheet music is available for purchase at your studio
- Whether you prepare students for exams
- Whether or not your studio offers group lessons
- Whether you hold regular studio recitals
- Whether your studio has a waiting room
- Whether parents are welcome at lessons
- Whether your studio is air conditioned
- Whether your studio has recording facilities
- Whether you use music education software
- Any other relevant information

Addition extras

It's also possible to add a photo to your website, together with a scrolling news ticker that you can use to display breaking news in your studio—student of the week, upcoming recitals, theory brainteasers—whatever you like.

Ensuring your webpage works hard for you

Whether you have taken advantage of a free PracticeSpot studio webpage, or have created one of your own, simply *having* the webpage is not enough. You need to make sure it gets noticed by prospective students in the first place. Otherwise it's just another webpage amongst hundreds of millions of others on the internet.

So how do you do this? Simple really — your webpage's job is to promote your studio. Which means you need to take some steps to promote your webpage.

> **It will work for you 24 hours a day, 7 days a week, and provide a depth of information about your studio that your conventional advertising never could.**

Voicemail message

As the first impression of your teaching studio, your voicemail message is probably already more than just a "Hi — leave your message". Now you can also include your web address in that outgoing message, so that even if the prospective student wasn't able to catch you on the phone straight away, they can go and get more information about your studio anyway.

So the message would be something like:

Hi, this is Alison Smith, and the number for Smith Flute Studios. If this is an enquiry about music lessons, please leave a message, or visit my webpage at www.alisonsmith.practicespot.com"

From the webpage, they can probably find out the answer to their questions, and can also email you to arrange an interview.

Annex to Yellow Pages or newspaper ads

Yellow Pages or Newspaper ads can be tremendously effective, but the limitation of ads like these is always one of space — there's only so much you can squeeze into the inches you are paying for. However carefully you word the message, there will always be the feeling that there's plenty you had to leave out.

This is where your studio website comes to the rescue. Put a few attention grabbing points in the conventional print ad, and then make sure your web address is featured prominently. Once the ad has created curiosity for the prospective parent, your website can sell them on the rest. (Again, the very fact that you even *have* a studio website will impress prospective parents)

The end result? You can make *thousands* of words of information available to your reader, without having to resort to an enormous and prohibitively expensive advertisement. You just need to state "For more information, go to the studio website at (your address here)"

Your website takes over from there, providing a wealth of information about your studio that a printed ad never could.

Letterbox Drops

Your desktop publishing program and color printer can help produce impressive brochures for local letter box drops, and because the targets are all in your neighborhood, you have the instant advantage of being perceived as "nearby" for any parents who are looking for music lessons.

The only disadvantage is that plenty of other music teachers in your area will also be doing letter box drops — because it's cheap and easy for them too. You can help yours stand out from the crowd, because yours is going to feature a link to a website:

We're just around the corner, and you can get more information about the studio 24 hours a day at (your address here)"

The end result? Your competitors do their letterbox drop, and the only thing parents will know about their studio is what is contained in the brochure. Your letterbox drop provides access to much more information—together with the sense that your studio must be a little more established (it must be to have its own website, is how the thinking goes).

It's a little thing. But it's often a little thing that will help the readers call you instead of someone else.

Online discussions, newsgroups and email

Google or Yahoo newsgroups have plenty of thriving communities devoted to music lessons. You can take part in discussions—and help prospective students find you—by including your studio website address in your signoff for each message. (As long as you are genuinely contributing to the discussion at hand, this shouldn't be perceived as spam)

> **When potential students call, it's not about what you tell them.**
>
> **It's about what you *couldn't*. Your webpage takes up where the phone call leaves off.**

Be generous in your willingness to provides answers to questions from students and parents. You'll be surprised at how often those answers will come back in the form of enquiries. Similarly, you can set up your email client (usually Eudora or Outlook) to automatically sign off your emails with your name and web address—all helping to create an awareness that your site exists.

Online music teacher registries

There are several websites on the net that are extensive directories of music teachers. The student types in the area they live in, the instrument they want to learn, and the directory will provide the contact details of teachers who match. There are plenty of such directories to choose from (and PracticeSpot will be creating its own in the not-too-distant-future), but two you might like to try in the meantime are:

- www.teachlist.com
- www.musicstaff.com

How does this help? There will be a space where you can enter your studio website address. Most teachers leave this blank, because they don't *have* a studio website — giving you an immediate edge over the other "matched" teachers.

On your letterhead

Instead of simply displaying name, address and email, your letterhead can also now include your web address. Don't just use it for your studio correspondence though. Use it for *all* your non-personal mail — it's not guaranteed to bring thousands of students stampeding to your door, but it just may be that the person who received your mail notices the letterhead, and has a kid who is thinking of starting lessons.

Like all lotteries, you can't win unless you buy a ticket — and this ticket is free, and takes seconds to add to your letterhead template.

Telephone Enquiries

When potential students call, it's not about what you do tell them. It's about what you couldn't. Most enquiries only take a couple of minutes, making it tough to communicate everything that is great about your studio.

Once you have your own studio website, instead of just ending the call with "goodbye", the last thing they can hear from you is "Listen, if you have any more questions about all of this, you can find out just about everything you need to know at the studio website at..."

The very fact that you have a studio website in the first place will impress. (How many other music teachers can boast their own website?) And the information there just might help trigger an interview.

Your local music stores

They're a great place to advertise. Not because other music teachers go there, but because music *students* – and their parents – have to go there too. (They have to get their music, metronomes and exercise books from somewhere!).

A well placed advertisement with some tear-off strips featuring your webpage address will attract the attention of parents while they shop, and if the time should ever come for a change of teacher, it will help ensure that your name leaps to mind.

Submit to Search Engines

Successfully placing your website high on search engine searches is an art in itself, but one thing is sure – for the index based search engines such as "Yahoo", unless you submit your site, you won't be listed at all.

Take some time to visit the most popular search engines and discover whether or not it's possible to submit your site – if you can, you should.

What's next?

Your **studio web advertisement** is just the start. The next step is one that will astound prospective students at interviews:

Their very own **lessons progress webpage** – all at your studio website. **24 hour, 7 day a week support** for students as they practice at home, with a **chronicle of their achievements and history**. When most parents see what you're about to read, they simply won't believe you – and they'll wonder how they could ever think of having lessons anywhere else.

Offer 24/7 support to all students(!)

It's been pointed out elsewhere in this book that if you want to make your studio irresistible to potential students, you need to offer something out of the ordinary.

Well, the idea you're about to read is definitely out of the ordinary. In fact, it would have been completely impossible for the people who taught you—but it will mean that you can make a claim that will astonish parents who read your ad:

> **Each student's webpage exists to motivate, inform, organize and inspire them *between* lessons**
>
> **Show it off at the interview, and enjoy the astonishment.**

"24 hour, 7 day a week support for each student as they practice at home."

This is a tuition-fee-paying parent's dream—a teacher who can actually help their child get the most out of the time *between* lessons! In other words, you're going to provide round the clock help for everyone you work with...

...actually, *you* won't. But your website will.

Even if you know nothing about the internet, you better read the next few pages. You can then casually refer to all of these options when prospective students call, and you'll actually hear the astonishment in their voices.

As you read the next section, keep looking at it from a prospective student's point of view. How excited would *you* be if you had just been shown all this by someone who could be your teacher? And why would you want to go anywhere else?

How it works

It all starts by creating your very own **studio website.** It's free to set up, and only takes a couple of minutes — in fact we've actually built it for you already. All you have to do is move in.

First of all, go to the official PracticeSpot Press website at **www.practicespot.com**. Once you're there, with the click of a button, you can create your very own studio website.

This is not just the web advertisement you read about in the last chapter. This is a special website built by the PracticeSpot team that will allow you to run every aspect of your studio.

The idea then is that every student in your studio can have their **very own webpage** at your studio website — *a page only they can see.*

Each student's own webpage acts as a record of their achievements in music lessons, a source of information for their parents, and helps to ensure that they are well prepared for their next lesson.

So what's it for?

On their own page, students can record how much practice they do, send messages to you, or read messages from you. You can send them "stickers" when they do great work, they can view practice instructions, key points from last lesson, a list of upcoming deadlines, together with newsletters, repertoire records, performance histories...and lots more.

> **When grandma asks "How are your lessons going?", the first thing the student will do is show her their webpage.**
>
> **It's all there.**

When grandma asks "How are your music lessons going?", the first thing the student will do is show her their webpage. It's all there — a rich chronicle of everything they have achieved so far, and a herald of all that is coming up.

In short, the child's webpage exists to motivate, inform, organize and inspire them between lessons, so that they hit the ground running at the lesson itself.

When you take parents on a tour of what it offers, they simply won't believe you.

Here's what you can tell them.

What students will find on their webpage

All the following tools will be available on your webpage, although you can easily turn OFF any tools you are not planning on using (you can always change your mind and turn them on again at any time)

Message Center

Instant and convenient communication between your studio and the homes of the people you teach.

Students can **send messages** to you, and you can send messages to them. Everything from "good luck" before a concert, to reminders, lesson cancellations or theory quizzes — it's up to you, and there's no limit to how many messages you can send.

It's not email, so there's no spam. Any message you send will instantly appear on the webpage of your student, while any message *they* send will instantly appear on your own Teacher's webpage. (Again, only you can see that page)

Your Message Center allows you to send a message to an **individual** student, to a **group** of students all at once (e.g.. all your "Beginners" or your "Wednesday students"), or to the **entire studio.**

> **Students can record how much practice they do, send messages to you, or read messages from you.**

You can read some great ideas for getting the most out of your Message Center at:

http://www.practicepage.com/help/?page=messagecenter

So why do prospective students get excited about the Message Center on their webpage? Apart from such a network making your studio instantly appear sophisticated and professional, it reminds parents that you're serious about being available between lessons if they get stuck.

And from your perspective, you never need to be disturbed by phone calls from students again—instead you can reply to the messages at a time that is convenient for you. So the irony is that being this accessible for your students will result in *fewer* interruptions of your personal time.

Studio buddies

Allows selected students to **send messages to each other.** (You can choose which students are "buddied") Buddies can organize car pools, support each other through recital preparation, or encourage each other to practice harder as a team entry in your Practice Competition.

> **You can send them stickers for great work, they can view practice instructions, key points from last lesson, a list of upcoming deadlines...**

You can also use it to allow more advanced students to mentor beginners—letting them share tips and support before the beginner's very first recital, and then giving positive feedback afterwards.

You can read more about the Studio buddies feature at:

http://www.practicepage.com/help/?page=studiobuddies

So why do prospective students get excited about Studio Buddies on their webpage? It's all about community building, and helping students support each other—they'll know that if they come aboard for lessons, they'll be welcomed and nurtured by your entire studio.

Online Notebook

Everything they need to practice for the week ahead, right there on their webpage, together with the key points from their last lesson. For students, it's a fun way to find out what their job for the week is, but it's parents who really love this, because they can always see what's required.

And because it's a webpage, you can *change* their instructions midweek if you need to—if they run out of things to do, or couldn't get the book they needed, or sprained their left wrist.

...together with newsletters, repertoire records, performance histories and lots more.

So why do prospective students get excited about the Online Notebook on their webpage? Because it means that students and their family support-team are always clear about exactly what they are supposed to work on between lessons. For busy parents, who might not be able to attend lessons, it represents a window into what's going on. What do I practice this week? That's easy. Check your webpage.

Stickerbook

Especially for your younger students. Reward them for great work by sending colorful electronic stickers to their webpage. Select the name of the student, choose a sticker from our collection, type a caption and click "Send"

ZAP! Your sticker (and caption) appears instantly on the webpage of that student.

Unlike the stickers you use now, you will have an infinite supply, and sending them costs you nothing. We'll be adding fresh stickers regularly, and students can watch their own collections grow in their very own online stickerbook. You can turn off this feature for older students if you wish, and can read more about the stickerbook feature at:

http://practicepage.com/help/?page=stickerbook

So why do prospective students get excited about the Stickerbook on their webpage? Because it shows that you are not only serious about giving positive reinforcement, but that you're creative about how it's administered. The stickers end up being a running diary of all the good things that the student has ever done as part of their music lessons, and something parents can make a fuss about between lessons.

Performance Records

A comprehensive record of every performance each student gives — from their first beginner's recital to their Carnegie Hall debut.

Students can also record *details* about each performance — venue, audience size, works performed, result (if it was a competition), acoustics — helping the performance stay fresh in their memories for years to come, and helping advanced or professional students build a list of preferred venues.

So why do prospective students get so excited about Performance Records on their webpage? Because it's a great way for parents and students alike to be able to see just how much has been achieved in lessons, with the Performance Records acting as a chronicle of their finest moments.

Studio Calendar

Making sure your students are ready for their deadlines on time, every time. You can get a bird's eye view of the studio as a whole, or look up the upcoming deadlines for any individual student.

Students will see all deadlines that affect them on their own webpage. And better still, any deadlines they enter *will automatically update your own calendar.*

So if they find out about an upcoming talent night at school, they can enter it into their Studio Calendar, and it will update your own records straight away — meaning that you can greet them next lesson by asking them about it.

This feature also allows you to record personal deadlines (birthdays, tax returns, due dates for forms etc.)

You can read more about the Studio Calendar feature at:
http://practicepage.com/help/?page=deadlines

So why do prospective students get excited about the Studio Calendar on their webpage? Because it means they will never be ambushed by deadlines again, and know that you will also be well on top of their child's commitments.

Repertoire Records

Allows you or your students to record the details of every piece they complete — from their first lesson to their first concerto. A great way for students and their families to track their progress.

The Repertoire records also allows the recording of accurate timings, tonality, program notes, tempo etc. — making it a powerful tool for more advanced students who need to plan concert or competition programs.

So why do prospective students get excited about Repertoire Records on their webpage? Because it's a symbol that stagnation is something that's not even contemplated in your studio. The unspoken assumption is not just that those records exist, but that their child will quickly fill them.

Items lent

Who has borrowed what from you, and when it was due back. For teachers whose book and CD collections always seem to be shrinking, this will allow you to keep track of those items you lend students.

Reminders can be sent directly to the webpage of your students, allowing parents to keep track of this for themselves.

So why do prospective parents and students get excited about the Items Lent section of their webpage? Because it simultaneously conveys that you are a well resourced studio that is willing to lend items to students in the first place, but are well organized enough to be able to keep track of such things. In short, it sets up an atmosphere of support, but with expectations on the part of the student — not a message that parents will mind at all.

Studio Policy

Accessible from your student's webpage, and designed to head off possible arguments before they start. You can edit it at any time, and it's an easy way to help new families orient themselves to various rules you have in the studio.

So why do parents of prosepctive students get excited about the Studio Policy at their webpage? I'm not sure that they will — but it does mean that they will always know where they stand. The very fact that your Policy is accessible in such a location helps lend it an extra air of authority.

Scrolling News Ticker

All the latest news from your studio, right there on the webpage of your students. Announcements, reminders, "Student of the month" awards, competitions, quizzes — it's up to you.

You can also use it to welcome new students — help them feel special and part of the community that is your studio right from the very first day.

So why do prospective students get excited about the Scrolling News Ticker at their webpage? Simple — when they look at it, they'll see that it's packed with information about events and students, helping them perceive your studio as being a foundry of excitement, creativity and industry. (So make sure that it IS packed with information about events and students!)

Link Library

There are plenty of great resources on the internet for music students. As you discover them, you can add links and descriptions to your Link Library.

Those links will then appear on your students' pages.

So if you give your students a report to complete on Beethoven, you can include some great reference links right there on their webpage.

So why do parents of prospective students get excited about the Link Library on their webpage? Because it shows that your lessons go beyond mere notes, and that your studio provides a breadth as well as a depth of musical education.

Fee Manager

Online billing allows you to send paperless invoices to parents, as well as easily record payments, and track overdue accounts.

Why do parents of prospective students get excited about the Fee Manager on their webpage? It's a bit hard to get excited about invoices of any sort, but the fact that this can be all handled online, together with online receipts, makes your studio look professional.

Practice Stats

Allows students to record how much practice they do, so that you can help them to practice more efficiently. (In fact so you can help them get more done in *less* time-which is the idea at the heart of my second book *The Practice Revolution*, see p240). They enter the information into their own page, your own records are updated instantly.

This makes it easy to run practice competitions, and also for you to keep track of students who might be struggling a little. Again, it's about being able to make a difference outside of the lessons themselves — if a student starts their week by recording three days of no practice at all, it's time to send them a quick message asking them if they need any help, and reminding them of their goal for the week. (It's very hard to read a message like that without then going and doing some practice!)

Keeping on top of it all

Work out which tools you want to use — and then turn the rest off. All the features outlined above are available through your webpage, but that doesn't mean you have to use them all. If the only thing you want to do is use the Message Center, then so be it. You can turn features on or off at any time with a single click.

How to find out more:

This has only been a cursory introduction to what's possible with your studio website. To get some more great ideas, go to:

www.practicepage.com/help

Where to get more help

www.practicespot.com

The world's largest resource and idea website for music teachers and students

This book is just the beginning — it's actually completely *dwarfed* by a much larger resource that's both free and online 24 hours a day. The **official website** for PracticeSpot Press, PracticeSpot.com has quickly become the world's largest website for music teachers and students, offering more than a thousand pages(!) of resources and ideas, and attracting over 1.8 million hits every month from music studios around the world.

The content is free, and you can check it out for yourself at **www.practicespot.com,** but I've included some highlights on the next few pages so that you know why you are firing up your browser in the first place.

There will also be a permanent section at PracticeSpot dedicated to *The PracticeSpot guide to Promoting your Studio,* allowing me to add new articles and ideas without you having to constantly buy revised editions of this book. There are contact details at the site for feedback, suggestions, conference bookings and the like.

In short, if this book has been useful for your own teaching studio in any way, I'd love to hear from you. *The PracticeSpot guide to Promoting your Studio* has been the second publication from PracticeSpot Press.

There are lots more coming.

Some highlights from PracticeSpot.com

PracticeSpot Theory Sheet Center

The Theory Sheet Center is a huge and growing collection of free downloadable theory sheets. Simply choose the topic you need, select the drill type, and click "print". You'll never run out—you can print a million copies of each sheet if your wish. Alternatively, you can simply give your students the address of the sheet they need to complete for homework. They can print it out at home, complete it, and bring it to the next lesson.

You'll still actually have to teach the theory to your students—all we've done is make sure that the workbooks you need are only ever a mouseclick away.

The PracticeSpot Rhythm Gym

The Rhythm Gym provides a series of carefully graded and annotated rhythm drills, designed especially for students who find reading rhythms tricky.

Students can work with the drills directly from the webpage, listen to midi files of correct performances, or you can print them out to work on in the studio.

The PracticeGuide

Further help for students who need to practice, but just aren't quite sure what to do. Provides many of the practice techniques outlined in The Practice Revolution, but aimed at students and their parents. Around 45,000 words, illustrated throughout, and one of the most popular segments at the site.

The Web's largest dictionary of terms

Helps your students turn obscure Italian words into something they can work with. Over 1200 musical terms, making this the most comprehensive music dictionary on the web.

Most music dictionaries can tell you what "allegro"and "pianissimo" mean. But we didn't just want to cover the basics. We wanted our visitors to get an answer on any term, no matter how unusual. Terms Like "Ghiribizzoso". Or "Straccicalando". Or "Ungestüm". Simply type in the mystery term — searches take less than 0.1 seconds to find what you need.

The PracticeSpot Dictionary is also searchable in **reverse**, meaning that you can input an English word, and it will find musical equivalents, perfect for composition students.

Manuscript Genie

The Manuscript Genie provides an infinite supply of manuscript paper at a variety of different sizes. Simply choose the type you need, and hit "print".

Studio policies

Just in case you were wondering how other teachers do things, PracticeSpot has a collection of studio policies, all contributed by visitors to the site. Browse through the ideas, and then send in the policy your studio uses (We'd love to hear from you!)

Music Crosswords

You can solve, check or cheat your way through our collection of crosswords — all dedicated to the subject musicians know best. Crosswords also include timers, for students (or teachers!) who get competitive about these things.

The world's first online music psychologist

Because life can be complicated for musicians. Expert free advice from Lucinda Mackworth-Young, who is a leading Consultant in Psychology for Musicians. Everything from dealing with difficult parents, coping with performance anxiety to string quartets that can't get along. Also includes a link to purchase Lucinda's excellent book on the subject — "Tuning In".

Practicespot's Sightreading Central

Dedicated to students who would like to read a little better. Free printable drills, sorted by difficulty, together with tips for improving sightreading. Midi files are available for all drills so that students can hear what the playthrough was *supposed* to sound like.

Online scales manual

Designed for keyboard students, the Online Scales manual has all 24 major and harmonic minor scales — but this time represented graphically on *keyboards*, not on staves, so that students can easily see which finger goes where. They can print out the ones they need, and keep them near their piano.

"For Teachers" online magazine

A collection of articles especially for studio music teachers. When I'm not busy writing books, I'm busy writing articles for PracticeSpot — so if this book has proved useful for you, then chances are you'll find plenty of articles in the "For Teachers" section that will help too. Studio promotion, finding great repertoire, motivating students, creating studio awards...offbeat solutions to common problems.

Chord Wizard

A tool for students to be able to instantly look up the construction of any chord or scale, with 564 different types of scales alone represented. So the next time a student is wondering what a Eb Minor Major 7th with an added 13th is, they can see it for themselves with the appropriate notes highlighted on the virtual keyboard at the Chord Wizard. With thanks to Colm Mac Cárthaigh for giving us permission to use his brilliant script.

Notereading Wizard

Self-marking notereading drills. Randomly generated, so you'll never see the same drill twice, and able to test 7 different clefs. Also provides support for ledger lines and mnemonic based drills (e.g.. All Cows Eat Grass). Gives the student a review at the end of each drill of any questions they got wrong, together with what the answer actually should have been.

The Infinity Rhythm Reading Machine

Randomly generated collection of rhythm drills, and a good way for students to test themselves once they have graduated from the Rhythm Gym. Students can set the allowable elements within any rhythm (e.g.. rests, dots, eighth notes), and the Infinity Rhythm Reading machine does the rest. Capable of generating over 20,882,706 TRILLION unique rhythms, so it will be enough to keep you and your students busy for a while.

...and lots more

There's much more at PracticeSpot that hasn't been mentioned here, and the site is being regularly added to. Teachers who want to be informed about new features or articles at the site can subscribe to the PracticeSpot Newsletter (it's free!). And as new books come out from PracticeSpot Press (I have another couple in the pipeline as you read this), details and excerpts will appear at the site.

Our aim remains to be a worldwide focal point for innovation, support and inspiration for the great career that is music teaching.

Also by Philip Johnston

The Practice Revolution:
Getting great results from the six days *between* music lessons

The most ambitious guide to practicing ever undertaken— over 320 pages of what works, what doesn't, what *really* happens when students practice, and how to fix it. The Practice Revolution seeks to end forever the obsession with how *much* practice students do, and switches the focus to helping students get more done in less time.

"... first-rate. After reading only half the book, I believe it had a positive impact on my teaching....Consider both buying the book and stock in the company!"
Horn Call - Journal of the International French Horn Society

"...a great success...a valuable resource for studio teachers in its wealth of strategy and stimulus to creativity"
American Music Teacher

"...idea-studded book on the whole practice process... when that student leaves, it should be with the practice skills to work alone. Johnston has generously outlined hundreds of ways to do that."
California Music teacher

Not Until You've Done Your Practice

Not Until You've Done Your Practice is my first book, and contains many of the essential ideas found in *The Practice Revolution*, but was written with *children* in mind. Big print, short sentences and cartoon filled, it's designed for kids to read *with* their parents—a head start for families who want to be a little more involved in music lessons.

First published in 1989, it's now in its third edition, has quietly been one of Australia's best selling books on music for more than a decade, and I'm still proud to be able to say that there's nothing quite like it anywhere else in the world.

Not Until You've Done Your Practice!

The classic survival guide for kids who are learning a musical instrument, but hate practising

Philip Johnston and David Sutton

You can find out more about *Not Until You've Done Your Practice* or order your copy online at the PracticeSpot website (click on "Useful Products")

'The concept behind this book is so simple and so effective, so long overdue and so desperately needed, that it is hard to believe no similar book has been attempted."
Australian bookseller and publisher

For conference booking, seminars etc.

For all conference bookings, workshops, festivals or seminars, I can be either be emailed through the PracticeSpot website at www.practicespot.com, or can be contacted directly at:

Philip Johnston
PracticeSpot Pty. Ltd.

52 Pethebridge Street
Pearce ACT 2607
AUSTRALIA

philipj@practicespot.com

+61 (2) 6286 8889

Probably the only thing I love doing more than writing, playing and teaching is public speaking — whether it's to small groups, large conferences, radio or television. If the ideas in *The PracticeSpot Guide to Promoting your Teaching Studio*, my other books, or elsewhere at PracticeSpot seem useful for your upcoming event, I'd love to explore how I can help.

In the meantime, while you're reading this, I'm actually having a lot of fun putting together the next PracticeSpot Press book. Keep an eye on PracticeSpot itself for details. There's lots, lots more to come ☺

Official PracticeSpot Press Website

www.practicespot.com
Ideas and resources for great music lessons

The world's largest and most comprehensive website for music teachers and their students. Over 1,000 pages of free resources, together with information about other PracticeSpot Press Books.

Printed in the United Kingdom
by Lightning Source UK Ltd.
102634UKS00001B/250